TRANSFORMATIONAL LEADERSHIP

Trust, Motivation and Engagement

Dr. Edward J. Shelton, PhD

Order this book online at www.trafford.com
or email orders@trafford.com

Most Trafford titles are also available at major online book retailers.

Printed in the United States of America.

ISBN: 978-1-4669-5849-4 (sc)
ISBN: 978-1-4669-5850-0 (hc)
ISBN: 978-1-4669-5851-7 (e)

Library of Congress Control Number: 2012917561

Trafford rev. 09/26/2012

 www.trafford.com

North America & International
toll-free: 1 888 232 4444 (USA & Canada)
phone: 250 383 6864 ♦ fax: 812 355 4082

Preface

I became fascinated with leadership early in my career as a young Lieutenant in the Army. Newly commissioned as an Infantry officer I was fortunate to be assigned on the DMZ bordering North Korea as a platoon leader. Within the year I served under two company commanders, I witnessed tyranny, condescending communications and absolute disrespect. One was a hated leader, while the other proved to be calm, respected, caring and a great mentor. I questioned how two leaders who had attended the same leadership development program could have such disparity in style. When I departed Korea, I was determined to become a student of leadership and find the answer.

Thirty years later having served in various capacities such as an assistant professor at Penn State University, a junior HR executive and a senior HR executive in industry, I have more questions than answers. What I have learned is that effective leadership is not a secret and that the art of motivation, empowerment, commitment, meaningful engagement and trust is known and can be acquired. This book is a summary of lessons learned as well as the basic fundamental principles best described as Transformational Leadership.

Transformational Leadership is the most effective leadership philosophy across social, organizational and military cultures. This book describes Transformational Leadership based upon solid principles with powerful antidotes and examples. The principles described in chapter one are found throughout this book to emphasize that Transformational Leadership is a philosophy and a way of life to be studied and perfected.

In an attempt to explain the effectiveness of cross-culture that is unique to Transformational Leadership, I have prepared two chapters entitled, *Middle East* and *Military* explaining how all effective leadership can be found in any organization and culture around the globe.

Central to the theme of Transformational Leadership is the characteristics that set this preferred style apart from other leadership methods and practices. It defines effective leadership and the idea that the global leader is a servant who leads people to realize their own greatness through professional competence, high moral character, and service to others' interests. Readers will be able to review the correlations and similarities of motivation, engagement, empowerment and trust, core to Transformational Leadership.

Importance is placed on developing competent leadership within an organization as well as for self-improvement. Understanding the relationship between leader behavior and followers' commitment directly impacts organization success. Employees who are committed to the organization first trust and respect their boss by choice while those who are not committed to their organizations do not have respect for their boss.

Dr. Edward Shelton

Contents

Seven Principles of Effective Communication
Hearing Is Not Listening
Destructive Communication
Communicating Positively
Sincere Praise

Dark Leadership of Manuel Noriega
Senator Ike Skelton's Example of Character

Being Offended
Benedict Arnold's Betrayal
First Gulf War

Mid-Eastern Leadership
Culture and Religion
The Leadership of Umar ibn al-Khattab
The Leadership of Khalid bin al-Walid

Military Leadership
Lt. Murphy's Story

Chapter 1

Transformational and Transactional Leadership

Transformational Leadership has its roots with James Burns (1978) describing this leadership style as "Transformational Leadership is a process in which leaders and followers help each other to advance to a higher level of morale and motivation." After more than thirty years, research has validated Burns suggestion that Transformational Leadership is a partnership between the leader and the member, mutually supporting each other to a higher level of motivation. This interaction of engaging in each other's best interest has moral and ethical benefits that are inspirational for both parties, thus the term "transformational"; its nucleus is change and has a changing effect.

> **Transformational Leadership is a partnership to reach a higher level of motivation, trust, engagement and empowerment.**
>
> **Transactional Leadership is based on rules and transactions using rewards rather than inspiration and self-choice.**

Research suggests that over 88% of all leaders are transactional leaders while less than 12% are true transformational. Transactional

Leadership tends to align the leaders with their followers by meeting base needs or "transactions," or exchanges between leader and follower where both parties receive something of value. For example, the leader provides the employees with rewards such as promotions and pay increases in exchange for a level of loyalty and productivity by appealing to their self-interests. All is contingent on this reciprocal cycle of support.

Transactional Leadership, in this light, places emphasis on a rigid structure of rules that, when violated, are met with punishment or corrective actions. Transactional leadership tends to shift the responsibility of leadership accountability to the system rather to the leader. Transactional leaders use structure as motivators, relying on the desired effect that performance produces rewards, working within the organizational framework and following the status quo, reacting to problems rather than being proactive and creative is typical transactional leadership.

This is not to say that transactional leaders do not set or reach goals; they do, in most cases the job gets done but the difference is the methods used to engage with and motivate the followers. Transactional leaders use the organizational procedures and structure to motivate the followers to participate or to improve communications.

> **Transformational Leadership places emphasis on the relationship between the leader and the follower. These leaders place worth on the individual and his or her interests; it goes beyond the leader's self-interests.**

Transformational leaders do not totally discard the organization's hierarchal structure and programs, but, in fact, may strengthen them by working within structure and policies to build and expand new ones and collapse old ones.

Transactional leadership has its benefits in industrial or professional settings where flexibility, creativity and independent thinking and acting may not be advantages. An example would be a nuclear power plant that has been engineered and designed to function under strict protocols;

the slightest error could have catastrophic consequen[ces]
that some Transformational Leadership style is not a[...]
motivation and social benefits, but, in general, the safe[...]
the plant depends on a more transactional presence. C[...]
such as the military rely more on situational leadership that may call
upon both methods before and during operations.

Four methods used by transformational leaders

Charisma
Inspirational Motivation
Intellectual Stimulation
Individual Consideration

Transformational leaders have self-confidence that allows them to feel satisfied with themselves and direct their efforts towards allowing them to lead from strength rather than from uncertainty or weakness. Assuming that the leader's confidence is altruistic, Transformational Leadership allows the leader to operate from a base of fixed principles rather than making up the rules as they go.

Transactional leaders are like chameleons, changing the view to fit the situations, which tends to confuse associates and followers. Transformational leaders are those who lead the way and set the example, they are not long-distance leaders. Another aspect of Transformational style is that it creates a social network and leaders are not afraid to develop friendship-like associations with those they lead, often going counter to what transactional leadership considers fraternization like risks. However, this working environment, if processed properly, results in high levels of performance.

Transformational leaders listen without being condescending because they care for the individuals whom they lead. They do not attempt to deceive their members; they are honest in their dealings and candid with their communications. This sense of integrity and openness is derived from a genuine sense of caring and desire to improve the followers.

A distinctive characteristic of Transformational leaders is the showing of genuine concern for the needs of the member first, putting themselves second and at times go beyond what normally would be expected from manager/leaders.

True Transformational leaders will step above Maslow's self-actualisation to a level called idealized influence that sheds one's own needs totally, emphasizing the importance of being discerning with regard to others, without seeking to control them. An important aspect at this level is the concept of choice for the followers. Exercising choice frees the follower from pre-conceived ideas, policies and formats to extend their ideas and abilities (within certain altruistic guidelines) and fulfill their own needs, thereby creating a motivation that is hard to establish under normally rigid work environments.

Without choice there can be no real freedom and empowerment in the workplace for the follower. Transactional leaders, on the other hand, manipulate others for the need to use them for self-serving reasons. With a higher level of idealism, Transformational leaders develop a unique perspective for people and problems. They develop and respectfully select the proper language and approach that impact follower's long term.

Transformational leaders are confident with themselves, weaving transformational style into their very being—they live the principles not simply talk them. As a result, Transformational leaders become comfortable with whom they are and tend not to seek power or control, but seek to enable others to rise to if not surpass their own potential. Finally, effective leadership was once viewed as being able to impose one's will on the group rather than developing mutual respect with both the leader and the follower nurturing innovation, moving forward with one purpose being bound by higher values of trust and courage.

Transformational leaders not only trust their followers but are trusted by them as well. They are not afraid to share responsibilities or teach them higher skills that require the leader to delegate and empower followers, giving them important things to do for their development.

Transformational leaders do not feel that they have to do it personally in order to get it done right; they are eager to share responsibility as a teaching opportunity for their followers benefit and growth.

Transformational leaders see followers not for what they are now, but what they can become. While doing this, the leader understands the balance needed for followers' success and does not over-match them in relationship to their capacities. Followers are not overwhelmed with more than they can manage, but enough to stretch them and bring about personal growth and changes. Finally, the Transformational leader holds the followers accountable not only for their actions but for their development. Many well-meaning leaders protect their followers by withholding challenging assignments in order to avoid conflict or failure. Accountability is essential for development and change; Transformational leaders will set and communicate high standards, and followers tend to perform at a standard set by the leader. The major reason Transformational Leadership motivates followers is that it enhances self-worth. As the Transformational leader empowers and encourages the follower to tap into his or her own strengths, the follower is influenced by the role modeling propagating desired behaviors that not only benefit the follower but the organization as well.

A unique aspect of Transformational Leadership is the emphasis of moral responsibility to others, which is closely aligned with integrity. It is noted that Webster's definition for integrity: "The quality or condition of being whole, complete, unbroken and undivided." However, after that initial point of agreement there are much different views as to how it is applied. Integrity is a standard of goodness or rightness in human conduct. The problem with this view is that the defined conduct of executives can vary greatly as proved by the ever increasing establishment of organizational code of conduct, ethics standards and governmental controls such as the Sarbanes-Oxley Bill mandating accountability and ethical conduct within organizations.

Transformational Leadership depends on honesty and integrity to build upon its main strength of believability from the follower. Integrity means always doing what is right and good, regardless of the immediate consequences. It is always doing the right thing without thought, motive or design. It draws parallel to being perfect or near perfect. For business executives, it would mean being trustworthy and incorruptible and having a great deal of trust and confidence from the followers and customers.

Transformational leaders with integrity tend to develop capable subordinates who are motivated with challenging assignments and who are satisfied working in an environment that has purpose. Followers will emulate Transformational leaders who have strong integrity and can be trusted by the followers. Followers will feel the sincerity when the leaders encourage open communications and exchange of ideas without fearing reprisals or retaliation.

> **Transformational Leadership has a unique quality that reduces social loafing among followers and is beneficial to team development.**

Attempting to construct a framework for teams around Transformational Leadership has its advantages since teamwork processes are connected with performance.

Transformational Leadership has an element of altruistic design that sets examples to be emulated by followers. However, the notion of moral leadership can be rejected when dark leaders such as Hitler may have adapted transformational like leadership at times as did many other noted leaders in history such as Jim Jones and Manuel Noriega; the differences being the lack of altruism and an abundance of egoism. Transformational Leadership is built on genuine trust, praise, recognition, and empowerment to all levels of influence and is demonstrated by the leaders trust and confidence in the follower's ability.

Mentioned earlier, there are four components to Transformational Leadership: charisma, inspirational motivation, intellectual stimulation and consideration for the individual. One historical example of these components is reflected in the life actions of Abraham Lincoln, who confronted General Grant and Secretary of War Stanton before the end of the Civil War. Both men were bitterly criticizing Lincoln for his leniency that they believed was destroying the discipline of the army; they stated publicly that his disregard for disciplinary guidelines or "transactional style" would ruin him politically. Lincoln seldom let the critics get to him when making difficult decisions. For instance, one incident occurred that so embittered the military and most northern citizens at the time but is now viewed as a true act of compassion for the individual. A soldier's mother (printed later in the book), had pleaded with Lincoln to spare her condemned son from the firing squad; she had already lost three sons to the war, and this son was the last. Lincoln listened quietly and then produced a piece of paper instructing the boy to be released immediately to his mother. The generals were appalled when they learned that Lincoln not only pardoned the widow's son but also publicly declared, "I am unwilling for any boy under eighteen to be shot." Then, turning to his Secretary of War Stanton, Lincoln added, "I have never been sure but what I might drop my gun and run myself, if I were in battle. Anyway, I don't see that shooting will do him any good."

In today's business and political settings, it seems that pseudo-Transformational Leadership is everywhere. It dominates our news as leaders of major organizations are given prison terms for embezzlement, unfair trade practices and mismanagement. CEO salaries are climbing faster than ever before; greed and corruption abounds to the point where true transformational leaders seem to have become extinct. At every level we see corruption, serving self-interests while putting up a front of care and concern. The availability of news and information has brought these pseudo-transformational leaders to the public more so than ever before, undermining those leaders who do seek the best for the most. Unfortunately, this availability of news seems to fan the flames of those to-be-leaders who carefully watch and learn how not to get caught and perfect the art of deception and greed.

Effects of Transformational Leadership

The ability of leaders to effectively practice transformational style can be instrumental in implementing strategies such as communications, team development, recruiting, training and culture building. Dvir, Eden, Avolio and Shamir conducted a study to test Transformational Leadership's impact on followers. The results of the study suggested that Transformational Leadership does have a positive impact on performance and individual development, while transactional measures were negatively related to business goals and objectives.

Six key behaviors associated with Transformational Leadership that contributes to organizational effectiveness:

> **Inspires others with a shared vision for the future**
> **Leads by example**
> **Encourages employees to work as teams**
> **Sets high standards**
> **Is respectful of individual feelings and differences**
> **Is intellectually challenging**

When these behaviors can be applied with consistency, the followers recognize that their interests are important and that the organization depends not only on their bodies but also on their minds and skills. They become motivated and, to an extent, self-actualized as they realize their needs for recognition and appreciation as individuals come first.

Organizational leaders may often take a for-the-moment transformational approach that rolls out new goals and visions to the workforce by, first, announcing there is a change in the way business is doing, to include participation and better communications second, creating a separate division or department to design and push the vision down and through; third, using consultants as experts to gather information and ideas from the workforce and organize them in PowerPoint form; fourth, conducting special off site seminars to share with upper managers what the consultants have found and openly discuss new strategies and goal paths; finally, meeting in one year to see how things are going, only to find that it was nothing more than a great pep talk and cheerleading event.

These approaches fail because the CEO and top leaders make no effort to change their behavior and become examples who are devoted to building commitment. These cycles of pumping up the organization create a dangerous environment characterized by confusion, bitterness and cynicism.

Transformational Leaders have more success in meeting organizational goals characterized by high optimism and self-efficacy. These Transformational Leaders achieve organizational goals through the concerted efforts of others; they know how to us human assets and how to motivate and direct them. Managers with a transformational style utilize the full range of behaviors such as individual consideration, intellectual stimulation, inspirational motivation and idealized behaviors.

> **Researchers have linked Transformational Leadership with team building effectiveness and group performance.**

There is a link between Transformational Leaders and group effectiveness by positively affecting team processes including cohesion, communications and conflict management. Building teams that can perform in harmony can better serve the organization by reducing turnover, improving morale and bringing collective knowledge into the problem solving process.

No other area has benefited from the Transformational Leader more than America's high tech industry. The need for creative/innovative workers in the high-tech industry is greater than ever and keeping those workers can be challenging. Netflix, HP, Google, Abode Systems and SanDisk, to name a few, depend on creative high skilled laborers to keep new product designs on the cutting edge for market security. These are workers who bring the skills and knowledge to organizations in a highly competitive arena. Their work environment does not include micro management or rigid transactional systems. Losing these workers comes at a high cost and loss of intellectual capital that competitors are eager to obtain.

> **Transformational Leadership provides a creative environment, motivation and opportunity to apply skills in a way that benefits their needs as well as the organizations.**

A firm's competitiveness may be at risk if the leader engages in unethical practices or has a low level of virtue and moral character. Yet leaders, who appear as transformational, may engage in unethical practices such as stealing money for their own use or misusing organizational assets for gain.

Can transformational leaders be self-serving yet pursue both the interest of the organization and their followers? Charismatic leaders, (similar to transformational), could participate in deceptive practices of Transformational Leadership, but with different motives. These leaders demonstrate characteristics such as narcissism, flawed vision and need for power; they encourage dependency on the leader rather than independence, choice and lack of internalization of values and beliefs.

Authentic Transformational Leadership provides a more reasonable and realistic concept of self a self that is connected to friends, family, and community whose welfare may be more important to oneself than one's own. The distinction can be found by adding "authentic" to define Transformational Leadership in an ethical context.

Transformational Leadership embraces ethics and virtue in order to adhere to its implied characteristics, measured by observable results and actions as viewed by the followers. Only Transformational Leadership benefits the organization by developing and encouraging common interests between follower and organization. They do it as moral agents, seeking to expand the individual lifting them to higher levels of achievement while creating fairness and equity in the system.

At the same time, the organization is insured of good unbiased information, honesty in its systems and processes and an effective check and balance as workers become empowered to speak freely, quickly exposing practices that may be unethical or illegal.

Change will have an impact upon how leadership is defined, foiling any attempt to find the grand theory of leadership applicable to all. Scholars will continue to search and develop systematic ways of keeping the latest information in front as a collection of knowledge allowing for paradigm shifts in leadership theory.

Organizational performance is affected by five fundamental factors:

> **Model of Motive**
> **Leadership Styles**
> **Organizational Environment**
> **Culture**
> **Job Design**
> **Human Resource's Policies**

Transformational Leadership influence consistently emphasizes that:

Organizational Success

> **Good Communications**
> **Employee Empowerment**
> **Knowledge Sharing**
> **Good Morale**
> **Trust and Confidence in Management**

Leadership is the pillar on which human assets plug into the organizational mission; it is the worker who will drive organizational success. Leaders who ignore cultural factors among workers lose the benefits of those workers mental and collective value.

Leaders at all levels can help usher out the old ways of thinking regarding a "one size fits all" approach and use cultural differences effectively to usher in a new paradigm that fosters participation, empowerment, learning, and personal growth.

Transformational Leaders are part of a larger strategy that begins with their recruitment and selection, to effective mentoring and development under pre-selected organization leaders who take a long range view and commit the time and resources to build a strong leadership base at all levels and reward those who are truly transformational, while eliminating those who are not.

Transformational Leadership is the choice of style for the future, and while it may shift in terms of focus and direction, it is the most desirable style that will focus on human capital, harnessing the collective knowledge and talent to place the organization on the cutting edge of competitive advantage.

Transformational Leadership and Organizational Effectiveness

Distributing knowledge allows the organization to harness the collective creativity, skills and talents of the workforce, to empower them in becoming a partner with the business and to develop competencies that build competitive advantage. As partners in the organization, once followers were empowered, understood the vision, and brought into that vision, they would enhance the actions to insure that it was carried out, knowing that ultimately it would provide value to all those who were affected. A key difference is in the ability of followers to identify with the organization rather than be rewarded or punished for their participation or non-participation. In this example of power sharing, organizations utilize human assets to bond with organizational goals and objectives.

Teams must be empowered by management to lead and direct the affairs of change at the lowest level, and their style may or may not be predictable. Leaders who empower their workers and who lead others to lead themselves call the management style "super leadership." This applies to both leaders designated by the organization as well as informal leaders who surface during these initiatives.

The relationship between managers and workers has been reshaping for several decades. Manager-employee relations are now seen in terms of coaching, mentoring and facilitating. The division between the two roles at time may seem blurred, but they are still defined with purpose. The outcome, however, is designed to tap into the minds and mental knowledge of workers, giving them, in many cases, freedom to act independently, making choices regarding equipment purchasing, scheduling, inventory control and quality.

Employees are now in charge of tasks that once were reserved for management or specialists. This empowerment requires leaders who are able to foster a work environment and not fear encouraging employee participation in the workplace.

Empowerment Five-Factor Model

Extraversion
Agreeableness
Conscientiousness
Emotional Stability
Intellect (openness)

Transformational Leaders effectively use agreeableness, extraversion and openness towards their followers. These trait behaviors tend to strengthen the empowerment process by building trust, which is essential and prerequisite for true empowerment. Transformational Leaders build a strong bond of trust and respect as result of honest exchanges that characterize agreeableness.

Trust

The importance of trust is a factor that defines empowerment in a workplace that is becoming more diverse. Bringing this diversity together in a way where workers of different cultures and backgrounds can feel comfortable working with one another and experience commonality requires mutual trust.

The increase in the use of participative management styles and the emphasis on work teams have led to a focus on researching trust. The increased interest and reliance on teams and employee empowerment has increased the importance of trust as management control mechanisms are reduced and interaction increases.

Another factor in developing trust is the trust workers have with their immediate supervisors. This trust, often referred to as interpersonal trust, develops over time, resulting from day-to-day interactions between the two. Trust in the workers' supervisors as friends enables them to become more innovative and satisfied with what they are doing with the group, thus less likely to leave the organization.

As trust is established or re-established, organizations depend on empowering the workforce as a way of increasing decision making at low levels in the organization and enriching the employee's work at the same time. Leaders play a critical role in creating the environment for empowering experiences for their subordinates: "The interpersonal work climate created by managers for their subordinates, contributes directly to subordinates feelings of self-worth and sense of determination."

> **An organization which has difficulty in gaining the trust of its employees will also experience difficulty winning the trust of investors.**

Trust can be reflective in its member and can be impacted by unethical practices of top leaders, reduced benefits, excessive changes in management teams and lay-offs. The connection between members' trust and shareholder value was strong, employee commitment leads to positive shareholder returns. Creating empowered workers begins with trust in leadership, and within the work groups itself.

Empowerment

> **Empowering the workforce can diminish in organizations that have too much bureaucracy and where, any if not all, decisions are minimized by those at high levels.**

This tampering down has impact on trust that members have for the organization overall, not to mention that of the leader with whom they deal. Effective empowering by organizations must develop a tiered structure of decision-making that is defined and understood before empowerment strategies are developed and implemented.

Another key element in empowering the workforce is how information is made available to the members. Employees who have knowledge concerning the organization's direction will have ownership in proportion with the information allowed to be. Combining knowledge and information with participation on that knowledge strengthens employee empowerment by sending a message that the worker is an important asset to the organization and that their efforts have an impact. Not only is job satisfaction at issue for members, but that the interaction and interest shown the member by supervisors and other team members are critical in determining the level of commitment to the organization.

Empowering people results in work satisfaction, commitment and job performance. It also strengthens the relationships between supervisor, co-workers and other levels of management within the organization.

> Transformational Leaders enhance feelings of self-value and empowerment. They express confidence in subordinates, set high standards, promote opportunities for participation in decision making and set inspirational or meaningful goals. They look after the individual's interest and happiness to ensure that these individuals are being fulfilled and can attain success whatever their level of performance might be.

The professional hierarchy does dictate the selection of the leader—the physician in primary medical settings, the engineer in project management settings—but unfortunately, these individuals, whether by training or temperament, may not be the person best suited for leadership. This applies to nearly every organization existing today; there seems to be a trend in business to select the most task-oriented worker and place him or her in a leadership role in hopes that he can make the other members like him. These task-oriented leaders tend to lack certain qualities necessary for team development and employee empowerment. While they tend to be effective at short-term results, they do not often have the foresight to set long term goals. They may not see the necessity of building alliances or developing interpersonal relationships in getting others involved with the process.

> Empowerment includes open communications which can be seen as a threat to the good order of things, and certainly consensus among the group might seem like a weakness.

This pro-transactional leadership view is a common problem that organizations face. Transactional-based leadership focuses on the institutional systems and processes that are designed to comply with administrative requirements. It centralizes power and control at the top of the hierarchy, causing dictates of information, policies and procedures. Transactional methods do not push responsibilities, power and influence to the workers, making it difficult to organize for self-directed or empowered teams and members.

Transformational Leadership plays an important role in successful team development and implementation. Transformational leaders instill motivation and stimulation within the group; this includes idealized influence or charisma, inspirational motivation, intellectual stimulation and consideration for the individual. The individual team member is coached and mentored, whether by another member or the leader, based upon the individual's needs and capabilities. Transformational leaders understand the inner motivations of the follower and then seek to satisfy those needs. The leader sets high standards and motivates the followers to heighten their awareness of the importance and value of the outcomes and methods of attaining goals, getting them to transcend their self-interest for the good of the group.

Creative workers are more stimulated to create when their motivation is enhanced. Transformational leaders focus on inspiring and motivating followers by challenging them to achieve a level of performance and productivity beyond what is anticipated. In order to do this, teams themselves must feel empowered.

> **It is not enough to say that they hold power but they must witness senior management keep hands off position as they make contributions to the organization without unreasonable interference.**

Leaders going forward will need to be more capable, smarter and encourage innovation. Getting everyone involved will be critical as a management philosophy. Organizations such as Microsoft, Walt Disney Company, Google, and GE encourage all employees to participate in presenting ideas up the organization in a variety of ways, including organized teams, social events, suggestion programs and other creative systems designed in part mainly by HR.

> **"The person who figures out how to harness the collective genius of the people in his or her organization is going to blow the competition away"**
>
> **CEO of Citibank, Walter Wriston**

Transformational leaders can promote employee empowerment by demonstrating benevolence through genuine consideration for employees' needs and interests and by protecting their rights. Transformational leaders do not exploit their members for their own interests, and they do follow a communications strategy that is honest and open. They gain the employees' trust and confidence by sharing control of both the work tasks and knowledge allowing the members to participate in the decision-making process.

Leaders who have a transformational style and who have the respect and trust of the members will enhance the creativity, productivity and efficiency of each member, who in turn strengthen the team as a whole. Senior management view transformational leaders as valued members who form work teams or groups that contribute to the organizational goals and gain legitimacy and continual resources to continue their efforts.

18

Organizations with Bad Leadership

> The best way to describe a manager in crisis is to describe a manager who excessively worries about himself or herself; has lack of purpose and courage; has a weak commitment; does not trust anyone or anything, and moves too slowly to make decisions'.
>
> Employees are in desperate need of an effective leader, or, more specifically, a leader whose influence is perceived as being highly correlated with high levels of employee satisfaction.

A leader who has self-respect, sets high standards, and individualized consideration demonstrates the comparison between a weak and a strong leader and the impact that leaders can have on the organization. Not only does Transformational Leadership motivate the followers to give extra effort, it has a pro-active quality, fosters self-esteem and promotes achievement-oriented behavior.

> Transformational leaders have more project success. This can be attributed to the transformational effect on followers by providing meaning and challenge, by arousing enthusiasm and by applying relationship-building qualities to the group.

Transformational Leadership has an inspiring and empowering tendency, creating an environment of excitement to pursue the organizational goals. The fostering and embracing of the organizational goals and aligning them with the personal values of the member of the group are critical to team building and organizational effectiveness.

Transformational Leadership style affects the organization in general more than any other style. Transformational leaders provide a group that is cohesive, motivated, performance driven, and committed.

Organizations moving forward will face challenges characterized by emerging competitive global markets, changing technologies, economic shifts, mergers, and a changing workforce. Organizations in the front will be those who can manage change, develop the workforce into an integrated system and develop vision that is extraordinary. Leadership will play a key role in defining how well the organization can break away from the traditional structures and concentrate on strategic priorities such as using strategic vision, empowering employees, accumulating and sharing knowledge, gathering external information and challenging the status quo.

> **In the future Millennium leaders will understand their followers, how they feel, what their needs are, what level of training and skills they have, and what concerns they have.**

Finally, Transformational Leadership is positively related to both the combination and exchange of information. This finding is not surprising, considering that the intellectual stimulation of followers is a core attribute of the transformational leader. Transformational leaders stimulate followers' efforts to be creative and innovative by questioning their assumptions, and by getting them to approach old problems in new ways. By encouraging team members to come up with and share new ideas and ways of tackling problems, the Transformational leader can help to facilitate the combination and exchange of information.

Leadership and Culture

Within the past three decades, global workforce diversity is the key driver for organizations human capital. With the dependence on labor and the global economy becoming stronger and more competitive, the ability to harness workers' talents, commitment and knowledge will separate those organizations that can survive from those which will succumb to cost and quality.

The need to provide effective leaders who can apply those characteristics that are effective in utilizing knowledge and human capital within the framework of cultural diversity will be in demand. However, the leadership style that is effective in the American culture may or may not be effective to Asian or Middle East culture and the search continues in boardrooms to define the most effective leadership methodology

Research from Gert Hofstede states that culture does have impact on how subordinates react to leaders, which does, in turn have an impact on organizational dynamics. There are two differences of thought regarding culture and leadership; one thought is that leadership is driven by a universal set of principles and is similar across cultures, while other scholars view leadership as being driven and directed by culture.

> **Universal tendencies are found between cultures and that certain positive leadership factors are found that motivate across cultural barriers. Transformational Leadership effectively crosses cultures.**

Understanding culture can best be viewed from six principles that form the foundation of cultures:

1. **Collective agreement**
2. **Common interpretations and meanings**
3. **Common norms and shared cognitions**
4. **Common history, language and to some extent religious affiliation**
5. **Passing on of defined patterns to following generations**
6. **Expectation of conformity within the group**

Transformational Leadership is recognized as a preferred style for global operations that depend on cutting edge results and high performance from the workers. Getting these results requires effective organizational development of its leadership program that provides a leadership pipeline within the organization that is sustainable.

Chapter 2

Leadership Development and Competency

The importance placed on developing effective leadership is important because, the relationship between leader behavior and follower commitment and trust directly impacts organization success. Literature suggests that employees who are committed to the organization are first committed to their boss's and the correlation is clear, they love their bosses while those who are not committed to their organizations do not respect and are on the verge of hating the boss. While the love hate relationship is not always on the extremes, it does fall within a spectrum that may best be described as effective to ineffective.

Need for Effective Leaders

In the global economy, there is a struggle to compete as more companies enter the markets and mergers continue at a faster rate than ever before. There is also a rise in ethical failures as organizations that once were successful thriving and on the cutting edge of their particular industry face a workforce that is less dedicated and committed. Today's leaders are un-focused, poor decision makers; while ambitious, they drive the bottom line, seek their interest or that of a select few at the top, they fail to set examples which results in the fact that they cannot sustain nor guarantee organizational success.

Leaders become fixed in their actions, on the equipment, their investments and focusing on their success so much that they forget the most important asset they have, their people.

"If your organization is undergoing tremendous success remember, it guarantees nothing for the future."

Your success will hinge on how you develop your front line leaders, they will take you to the cutting edge and keep you there if you have trained them as leaders who can inspire, develop trust and successfully get the people to eagerly participate in the entire process.

Most Workers Do Not Find Their Boss's Inspiring

Ten Percent of employees, to include the military, describe the relationship between management and labor at their organizations as "extremely positive."

Forty nine percent describe their relationship as "lukewarm to negative."

Ninety percent strongly felt that their organizations did not listen to or cared about the workers

Ninety percent do not trust their bosses to look out for their best interests.

Interpreting the data suggests that 90 % of leaders lack the ability to fully motivate, inspire, and gain the commitment and respect of those who follow them.

6 traits of bosses that do not motivate inspire or gain commitment

Fail to keep promises.

Invade employee privacy.

Fail to give proper credit.

Blame others to cover up mistakes or minimize embarrassment.

Make negative comments about employee to other employees.

Give workers the silent treatment.

Most exit interviews at organizations with high turnover, (10% or more), reflect that the reason they are leaving is because of their boss. With this information in hand, it is hard to understand why organizations do little about it. Most recent polls of executives and presidents of companies, when asked which factor are the most crucial to the business, the top answer is always; retaining key workers and hiring qualified workers.

People don't leave their job or company; they leave their bosses.

Retaining and keeping good workers is rated above all other concerns such as developing new products, increasing productivity, upgrading technology, expanding markets, finding new finance and cutting costs.

Reasons for leadership disconnect

Lack of trust for their leaders

Lack of recognition and praise

Poor communication

It can best be summed up as having a lack of human relations practices and lack of common sense (poor judgment).

These findings are not surprising since management and consultants have acknowledged these problems for decades now. At the same time that top executives acknowledge that people are the most important assets they have, and that good employees are in short supply, why do they allow for those key leaders under them, effectively drive those very workers away?

The answer is both complicated yet simple, people want effective leadership. The complicated portion of this question has to do with the individual leader's behaviour and attitudes which of all assets within an origination, is the hardest to change and form.

The leader's practices and views define the organization's culture and the expectations of the organization in terms of employee behavior, customer service approaches' and other practices. The leader's constructed culture becomes ingrained in the organization, and often, over time the practices and values are not challenged or questioned, therefore, it becomes important to understand that leadership style does impact organizational effectiveness. Two ways to improve ineffective leadership styles and skills at this level or at any level is through self awareness leading to change or effective ongoing training by the organization.

Leadership is 50/50—50% is inherited while 50% can be learned. The best leaders make leadership a lifelong process of learning.

When there is emphasis on leadership development, it is often focused at the top tier, but seldom goes much farther down. Yet no matter how successful a leader is at the top, it means nothing if there are not effective leaders at the front line—in direct contact with the employees, who understand and share those same characteristics and abilities in proportion to their assigned responsibilities.

The best development of leaders is found in organizations that keep it in house and continuous. It takes a minimal of five years of continuous leadership development to develop competent front line leaders, ten for mid-level leaders and fifteen for strategic senior leaders. Leadership development within the organization usually is the role of Human Resources and must include training, mentoring, coaching and continuous accountability.

> **One Global Organization constantly recruited consultants to help design and build an elaborate program to develop front line leaders. The fees for their work exceeded half a million dollars per year, not considering the lost time off the job of those who participated.**
>
> **After 18 months, a meeting was held with the president of the organization in which after two hours, the president rose from his chair, stating, "I can't see one change to this organization, no, not one. We are at the same point that we were two years ago."**
>
> *Global Oil Company Executive*

The experience illustrates some flaws in this approach to developing leaders. The organization did its best, using the latest teaching methods to better its leaders and make a difference for those who participated. There were some short-term benefits, new ideas, critical thinking opportunities, and exposure to new tools. What the president of the organization saw, though, was that there was no evidence of permanent improvement in the organization or that the participants were better leaders than before.

The problem did not have its roots in insufficient effort or financial support. The problem was the relationship between the cost and the result. The president saw a disparity between what was being spent and the return on the investment, as result the leadership development training had not been effective. The top leadership had realized some benefits, but the benefit had not penetrated down into the organization, to the front line leaders or the followers. The failure was caused by lack of ownership, follow-through and accountability.

In more than 25 years working with leaders in the military, in academic halls, and in business, I see the challenge facing leaders are:

Engagement

Follow through and sustainability

Accountability

I would like to share an incident that happened many years ago, in another organization, as I was training a large group of front-line managers on leadership principles. This incident helps to underscore the earlier president's concern for effective training.

Leadership is a Learned Philosophy

> **While conducting a Front Leaders course, I had just finished discussing the principles of motivation, commitment and engagement when a participating manager raised his hand and in all sincerity asked, "Have our bosses attended these courses"?**
>
> **A problem in many organizations is that leaders stop studying the art of leadership and revert to reaction behaviors that are outside of best leadership practices.**

A well-known military concept is the philosophy, "Train everyone to lead." If every level is trained to lead, a hierarchical organization melts into a series of high-performing small units where change is managed with creativity and flexibility, and risk-taking can benefit the organization as front-line leaders are empowered to make innovative decisions even though they may never hold a formal leadership position in the organization.

If we know the principles of effective leadership and so much money and resources is put into leadership development, then why are we failing in developing effective front line leadership? Reasons often include lack of commitment from the top, not understanding behavior and learning methodology and finally lack of follow-through and accountability.

Every effective leadership development course that I have participated in or designed took a minimal of 5 intensive years to produce Transformational Leaders.

Do not expect effective front line leadership development with a onetime familiarization course or seminar. Effective preferred leadership style is a behavior that is developed and trained for over many years of continuous application and feedback cycles. The graph above is explained below:

Training Cycle for Front Line Leadership

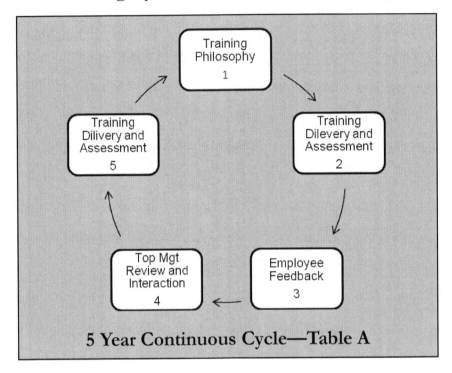

5 Year Continuous Cycle—Table A

Training philosophy (1) Table A senior management defines and explains what is expected of leaders, it defines how they will act, how they will communicate and describe preferred methods of leading. This leadership philosophy is packaged and delivered (2) in a continuous series of presentations starting with a basic awareness that describes preferred styles and fundamental leadership principles. Before or during this training and development, the organization must implement an assessment tool that is used to measure leadership skill level and developmental needs for the future. After a period of time, 3 to 4 months, and the organization conducts employee feedback (3) sessions by a champion third party (HR) who focuses on the quality process of leadership development and on application of principles by the front line leader.

The feedback is to determine if what is being taught being applied at the front line. It is important to note that this feedback is not to beat up the front leader but rather to help build and guide the leaders. This feedback (4) is reviewed by the upper most management who then gathers all his leadership together (once a quarter) to express what he sees as trends, weaknesses and strengths. He encourages and outlines leadership expectations of the organizations. The tone of these meetings must be one of encouragement, challenge and uplifting in language as well as accountability.

After a period of time (6 Months or earlier), the front line leaders attend another session of leadership development delivery (5) that reviews the leadership philosophy but also is used as an open forum to review employee feedback and used to help develop techniques and reinforce effective leadership principles. This session of training encourages further application of effective leadership and provides an open forum for discussion.

The cycle continues with ongoing employee feedback, upper management review and participation, continuous training forums for development and requires accountability for those who cannot meet the leadership challenge. This cycle takes a minimal of 5 years preferably 10. Without such a cycle, leadership development becomes simply a nice day away from the office.

Defining Leadership

Understanding leadership at all levels, it is important to identify the fundamental differences between management and leadership and those principles that are essential for all leaders to understand.

Management deals more with complexities and the process of planning, organizing, directing, controlling and coordinating resources that lead to achieving organizational goals. Leadership is more complex and involves relationships with people.

Leadership is directing change, its active, its interpersonal—true leaders inspire, have vision, set directions, enable people to extend their capabilities and ultimately inspire loyalty and command respect. Effective leaders tap into the followers' soul and have them choose to give their talents and commitment to the leader. These precious choices are not to be extracted through fear or intimidation but rather simple desire and free choice. Leadership is a 50/50 split. 50% born with and 50% learned.

Levels of Leadership

Front Line leadership is face-to-face or first-line leadership. It generally occurs in organizations where followers are accustomed to seeing their leaders all the time: departments, units, to include the superintendent level. The front line leader's span of influence may range from a handful to several hundred people. Supervisors are in direct leadership positions more often than their Managers and other counterparts.

Front Line leaders develop their followers one-on-one and influence the organization indirectly through their followers. For instance, a superintendent is close enough to the employees to exert direct influence when he visits training or interacts with followers during other scheduled functions.

Front line leaders generally experience more certainty and less complexity than organizational and strategic leaders. Mainly, they are close enough to the action to determine or address problems. Examples of direct leadership tasks are monitoring and coordinating team efforts, providing clear and concise organizational intent, and setting expectations for performance.

Organizational Leadership

Organizational leaders influence several hundred to several thousand people. They do this indirectly, generally through more levels of followers than do front line leaders. The additional levels of subordinates can make it more difficult for them to see and judge immediate results. Organizational leaders have staffs to help them lead their people and manage their organizations' resources. They establish policies and the organizational climate that support their subordinate leaders.

Organizational leaders generally include leaders at the Administrative Area through the Vice President level. Their planning and mission focus generally ranges from two to ten years. Some examples of organizational leadership are setting policy, managing multiple priorities and resources, or establishing a long-term vision and empowering others to perform the mission.

While the same core leader competencies apply to all levels of leadership, organizational leaders usually deal with more complexity, more people, greater uncertainty, and a greater number of unintended consequences. Organizational leaders influence people through policymaking and systems integration rather than through face-to-face contact.

Being Visible and Available

Getting out of the office and visiting remote parts of their organizations is important for organizational leaders. Make time to get to the field and to the remote sites to verify if their staff's reports, e-mails, and briefings match the actual production, the conditions their people face, and their own perceptions of the organization's progress toward mission accomplishment. Organizational leaders use personal observation and visits by designated staff members to assess how well subordinates understand the CEO or Presidents intent and to determine if there is a need to reinforce or reassess the organization's priorities.

An example of failed leadership due to lack of visibility was that of the Confederate President Jefferson Davis. Apart from two month-long trips across the country where he met a few hundred people, Davis stayed in Richmond where few people saw him; newspapers had limited circulation and most Confederates had little favorable information about him. The flaws in his personality and temperament made him a failure as the highest political officer in the Confederacy. His preoccupation with detail, inability to delegate responsibility, lack of popular appeal, feuds with powerful state governors, inability to get along with people who disagreed with him, and his neglect of civil matters in favor of military were only a few of the shortcomings which worked against him, but it was his inability to keep in touch with the front line that doomed his governance.

> **"The best leaders are those who do not isolate themselves from the workers or staff, they regularly are seen by all without medaling, people are a major source of information and have the knowledge and information of what's really happening."**

Having an open door and staying close to the people is a good model for leaders. I have adopted a practice of not depending on formal staff meetings to collect information, rather I try to make as much casual contact as possible, wandering around without meddling but finding out the facts for myself on key issues and have found it to be just as important as formal gatherings. I prefer to interact with people when they are in a more relaxed, less pressure packed environment and it has a value to the individual that they are important and I care about them. This contact gives leaders firsthand knowledge needed to make informed decisions without relying on filtered information in between, in fact it often times ensures that filtering does not take place between you and the front line workers as builds integrity into the flow of what is being reported to you.

Another impact of be visible and interacting with the workforce is that it builds confidence, encourages innovation, it allows you to teach and reinforce values and expectations and it is perhaps the favorite method of demonstrating the importance of transparency to those working around you. Accessibility has led many of those working for me to view me in a positive, trustworthy manner.

Strategic Leadership

Strategic leaders are responsible for large organizations and influence several thousand to tens of thousands of people. They establish the organizational structure, allocate resources, communicate strategic vision, and prepare the organization as a whole for their future roles.

Strategic leaders work in uncertain environments that present highly complex problems affecting or affected by events and organizations outside. The actions of a geographic manager and leader may often have critical impacts on local, regional or even global politics.

Strategic leaders apply all core leader competencies they acquired as direct and organizational leaders, while further adapting them to the more complex realities of their strategic environment. Since that environment includes the functions of all the organizations components, strategic leader decisions must also take into account such things as the organizations budgetary constraints, new systems acquisition, manpower programs, research, development, and inter-organizational cooperation.

Strategic leaders like front line and organizational leaders, process information quickly, assess alternatives based on incomplete data, make decisions, and generate support. However, strategic leaders' decisions affect more people, commit more resources, and have wider-ranging consequences in space, time, and political impact, than do decisions of organizational and direct leaders.

Strategic leaders are important catalysts for change and transformation. Because these leaders generally follow a long-term approach to planning, preparing, and executing, they often do not see their ideas come to fruition during their limited tenure in position. It is a complex undertaking that will require continuous adjustments to shifting political, budgetary, and technical realities. As the transformation progresses, the organization must remain capable of fulfilling its obligation to operate within the full spectrum of business operations on extremely short notice. While the organization relies on many leadership teams, it depends predominantly on organizational leaders to endorse the long-term strategic vision actively to reach all of the elements of the organization

Comparatively speaking, strategic leaders have very few opportunities to visit the lowest-level organizations in their organizational structure. That is why they need a good sense of when and where to visit. Because they exert influence primarily through staffs and trusted subordinates, strategic leaders must develop strong skills in selecting and developing talented and capable leaders for critical duty positions.

Developing Front Line Leadership

While this book is dedicated to the Front Line Leader, it is important to understand that good front line leaders nearly always make effective organization and strategic level leaders. These base leadership skills and competencies, if followed, are the formula that helps top tier leaders understands the power of delegation, empowerment and motivation. It is OK and allows leaders who possess these abilities mentioned above to lead people who are brighter and better than themselves.

Leadership entails boldness, venturing out to the cutting edge, leading from the front, and being susceptible to criticism. I imagine that everyone reading this book is a leader or has influence in the lives of others even if you don't realize it. My question to you and for you to seek out is what kind of leader are you or do you want to be? What kind of influence will you have on others?

Leadership Model

Has influence beyond work

- **Leads by example**
- **Communicates**
- **Inspires**

Develops

- **Creates a positive environment**
- **Perfects his/her skills**
- **Develops others**
- **Becomes a coach and mentor**

Gets Results

- **Inspires others to achieve**
- **Organization becomes better**

Chapter 3

Role of Leadership

If we believe that a leader's role is to inspire, have vision, set directions, and enable people to extend their capabilities and ultimately inspire loyalty and command respect. How is this achieved? Do we use fear as we have seen others do; or do we use kindness with a soft touch? The answer may surprise you.

There are many different techniques, principles and styles that can make a leader effective, yet allow for people to maintain their dignity and self-esteem.

No other story illustrates this better than from the view of a shepherd and the sheepherder.

The Good Sheppard

When I was a teenager in Italy, I lived near a field where a large flock of sheep grazed. Every evening, the sheep would be driven across the field and into the nearby mountain meadows for the night, by a man with a stick and his three dogs. As he walked behind the sheep, he would pound the stick on the ground driving the sheep forward, while the dogs yapped and nipped at their heels. If a sheep went the wrong direction, the man would strike the terrified sheep with his stick. He was a sheepherder.

> In contrast, several years ago in Mendoza, Argentina, I saw a great leader. He was fourteen years old at the most, his trousers were torn, he wore no shoes, and he was playing a musical instrument traditional to that region. There he was, flute in hand, playing and strolling leisurely in front of a flock of sheep, and they were following him. Every move he made, they made; he went left, they went left; when he would stop, they would stop. As they drank from the stream, he counted them to ensure all were safe, and then he drank last.
>
> There was no other compelling force to drive them; no stick, no dogs—nothing. They knew who their leader was and they trusted him.
>
> I haven't seen such a dedicated leader since.

What was the difference between the shepherd and the sheepherder? It was leadership. Leadership impacts every interaction of our lives, our family, work, government and our community involvement.

Leadership Is All About the Individual

The heart of leadership has to focus on the individual and his or her best interest as long as it is balanced, that is why it is important to understand how different styles of leadership affect those being led. Since you are dealing with people, not sheep, finding one grand theory of effective leadership that applies to all will be impossible. There will be as many different responses to your style as there will be people you are leading. And while there will always be scholars gathering and presenting their theories to explain this moving target—think "paradigm shift"—the truth is: Leadership is all about your relationship with the individual.

Effective leadership is the energizer from which human assets get their drive and productiveness, both on an individual basis and at the organizational level. This is especially true when working in a team environment. Human assets are simply . . . the people. Just as machinery, that is not maintained or is fed the wrong amount of energy, will break down or underperform, so goes it with your human assets. People—a much more important asset than machinery—need maintenance and attention, too, especially at the individual level. Unlike machines that work within a narrow, predetermined set of limits, people bring to the organization critical talents, skills, and precision that machines will never provide. The leader who ignores the importance of the individual loses the benefit of that worker's mental and collective potential

It has been my experience that leaders who understand the value of the individual are in demand at all levels. Organizations recognize these leaders and their ability to manage change and tap into the knowledge and talents of the workforce. These leaders are able to empower and motivate others, and this then becomes the choice of style for the future: to focus on the individual, and jointly, the people. While there may be shifts in concentration and/or direction, it remains the most desirable style. Then, by harnessing the collective knowledge and talent of teams of people, any organization will be on the cutting edge of competitive advantage. Understanding and applying this concept of the "individual", requires that a leader make a contract between him and each individual, of which he must be prepared to mentally sign, agreeing on the terms from the beginning. The contract must express the importance that they each become mutually supportive for the good of both.

It can best be summed up by Edmond Burke in his letter, *Reflections on the Revolution in France* (1790). He stated,

> **"Society is indeed a contract. It is a partnership in all science; a partnership in all art; a partnership in every virtue and in all perfection"**

Edmond Burke's comments provide a model for today's leadership; it is a reminder that the role of a leader is a partnership and moral contract that helps others to succeed. It is a race; not to win, but to achieve success for all. Achieving this partnership goal will depend on leaders developing in themselves and others a tolerance and understanding for differences in culture, for individual traits, and for organizational needs.

Five Principles of Partnership and Engagement

In order to have a true impact on others, leaders must embrace the following five principles upon which the partnership is founded:

Knowledge Sharing

Trust

Empowering Others

Building Teamwork

Building Team Trust

1. **Knowledge Sharing**—Sharing knowledge enables an organization to harness the collective creativity, skills and talents of the workforce. It acknowledges the importance of everyone's role as a partner in the business, and helps develop strengths that build competitive advantage. With knowledge, people feel empowered. When sharing the vision of the organization with everyone, individuals can then be encouraged to identify the connection between their actions and the organization's goals. Once brought into that vision, they can see how maximizing their contribution to the organization provides value to all those affected, including themselves. To be effective, all knowledge must be passed down to the first line operators.

People must identify with the group or organization and have a personal and deep understanding of what is going on and why. Sharing knowledge tends to do away with the need for rewards for participation or for punishments for non-participation. When most knowledge is common, a team-like atmosphere is created. There is little or no separation between those who "know" and those who "don't know," creating a deeper bond between members of teams, and between teams and the organizational goals and objectives.

However, building cohesive teams requires that management empower each member, and the team as a whole, to affect change at the lowest level. Teams must also feel free to exercise their creativity, and be given the information necessary to drive those changes.

Studies show that leaders who empower their workers, and who lead others to lead themselves, are not afraid to redefine their own role with the people by building relationships. They call this management style "super leadership".

The relationship between managers and workers has been reshaping itself for several decades. In many organizations that relationship is seen in terms of coaching, mentoring, and facilitating, so the division between a manager's role and that of the worker may seem blurred at times. There is still purpose in defining the different roles, but the more current processes, which tap into the minds and knowledge of workers, give them more freedom to act independently. In some organizations employees are now in charge of tasks that once were reserved for management or specialists. This empowerment requires leaders who are able to foster a work environment and not fear encouraging employee participation in the workplace.

2. **Trust**—Trust is built upon the leader's integrity, ability and benevolence, and is an important aspect in developing and maintaining workplace relationships, and communicating vision, helps to create the environment needed in order for empowerment to take place.

Anatomy of Trust

Integrity
Ability
Benevolence

The importance of trust as a factor that defines empowerment in a workplace is becoming more diverse. It requires mutual trust to bring this diversity together in such a way, that workers of different cultures and backgrounds can feel comfortable working with one another and experience commonality.

The use of participative management styles and the emphasis on work teams have led to a focus on researching trust. The increased interest and reliance on teams and employee empowerment has increased the importance of trust as management control mechanisms are reduced and interaction increases.

Highly effective organizations are characterized by a horizontal structure where task-oriented groups gather to work together on tasks, rather than as a vertical command and control structure. To succeed, there must be trust built among the members of each group, including trust that each will carry his or her own workload equally, and help bear other's burdens with genuine care.

The most important level of trust is between workers and their immediate supervisors. This interpersonal trust develops over time and results from day-to-day interactions between the two. Trust in his or her supervisor enables a worker to become more innovative and satisfied with what they are doing, and thus less likely to leave the organization.

As trust is established or re-established, organizations depend on workforce empowerment as a way of increasing decision-making at the lowest levels. Leaders play a critical role in creating the proper climate for successful empowerment, and to that extent, contribute directly to the enrichment of the employees' role in the organization, and to enhancing their feelings of self-worth and sense of determination.

Trust is so complex and deeply integrated into the collective success of an organization and of the individual, that a leader who has difficulty in gaining the trust of people will also experience difficulty winning the trust of others such as customers or investors. The connection between members' trust and shareholder value is strong; employee commitment leads to positive growth and return on investment. Creating empowered workers begins with trust in leadership, and within the work groups themselves.

3. **Empowering Others**—Empowerment means giving workers at all levels the knowledge, confidence, and authority to make important decisions. Effective leaders involve their people in the business process, and this empowerment leads workers to an enhanced sense of self-efficacy (one's belief that they can make a difference through their skills and talents). It enables those around us to take an active rather than passive role at work, and inspires people to do more than they thought they could do. Leaders who empower their people have enough trust in them to share some of the decision-making, which allows them to grow individually. At the same time they provide benefit to the organization.

Ineffective leaders tend to hold on to control and power, preferring to do everything themselves. Effective empowerment can be difficult in organizations that have too much bureaucracy, and where many, if not all decisions are made only by those at high levels. These executives have worked long and hard to get power, and they will not give that power up easily—plus they're afraid that workers don't know enough to make decisions on their own. Restricting employees' participation in this way has an impact on their ability to trust the leader with whom they deal, as well as the organization as a whole. An effective empowerment strategy must include a tiered structure of decision-making that is well-defined and understood by everyone before being implemented within the organization.

Another key element in empowering the workforce is how information is made available to the members. Employees who have knowledge concerning the organization's direction will have ownership in proportion to the amount of information shared. Combining knowledge and information with participation strengthens employee empowerment by sending a message that the worker is an important asset to the organization and that their efforts make a difference.

A leader who understands empowerment and delegation will let the people do everything within their power. He or she will stand in the background as a coach, fixing responsibility and then when necessary, providing instruction on how that responsibility is to be met. It is a continuous cycle. Give them freedom to do their tasks, never criticizing, but praising success and encouraging efforts.

When empowerment is done consistently, not only is a worker's job satisfaction improved and enhanced, but the level of commitment to the organization is increased based on the added individual attention given them by both their supervisor and other members of their teams. This strengthens the relationships between supervisors, co-workers, and other levels of management within the organization.

Empowerment

1. **Do not be afraid to delegate—then become a coach**

2. **Make the task seem exciting, challenging and important**

3. **Show others you have confidence in their ability**

4. **Give and show loyalty to people and expect it in return**

5. **Expect much from people and give much back**

6. **Follow people's progress; hold them accountable while still giving praise and direction in a spirit of concern**

7. **Allow people to change their work process**

8. **Allow people to make decisions involving money**

4. **Building Teamwork**—Your success as a leader largely depends on your ability to connect people to the organization so that collective knowledge can help drive organizational effectiveness. The development and use of teams allows organizations to compete in today's markets. Leaders in today's workplace must be creative; that is the base for change. It drives innovation and defines organizational effectiveness.

Driven to become more competitive, organizations have realized that the only way to achieve market advantage is to either lower wages, reduce material costs (meaning cheaper products), or design a more efficient organization.

Maximizing the individual worker is a strategy that can be built into a design for more efficiency. Workers today, are part of a group that is part of a larger social structure. Organizations can tap into a wealth of energy, experience, creativity and insight by accessing the collective knowledge and ambition contained within that group.

Research shows that 80% of Fortune 500 companies use teams as part of the operational process in their plants and processing areas. The popularity of teams with successful and reputable organizations demonstrates that this concept has become a strategic asset in today's business environment. It will become more refined in its design and impact, rather than diminish and fade away.

> **The best decisions are always made in groups—it takes more time—It is a difference between "we made the decision" and "I" made the decision. How can you fail?**

Utilizing a team approach results in a paradigm shift in how employees not only are viewed, but are treated as well. Another factor contributing to demand for employee empowerment and teams is the changing attitudes of the workers themselves. Employees want to participate and become integrated into the business operations of the organization. Workers have come to expect empowerment and participation and, in fact, if they are not motivated to be a part of the daily operation, will eventually cause the organization to suffer.

Things to be considered when designing a team include work design, composition, context and process. Literature suggests that people perform better when they are given opportunity to problem-solve, make decisions, listen, communicate both within and outside the team, and deal effectively with conflict. This is all made more challenging by their diversity. Developing these groups takes a dedicated management team who can monitor and supervise, yet knows when to be flexible and to let the team develop on its own.

One characteristic of an effective team is the high level of commitment of its members both to the organization and to the team. The stronger the team's interpersonal relationships, the greater the mutual accountability amongst the team members. Setting high standards of behavior for team members when dealing with each other, requiring honest yet respectful communication without fear of ridicule, accusation, or reprisal, can increase the level of trust, which is invaluable when creating and/or maintaining a good team. This eliminates finger pointing and fault finding, and leads to a greater sense of common purpose and commitment. Members respect each other and demonstrate mutual concern as each has the opportunity to grow, strengthening their level of trust not only in each other but also in the team system.

**"If everyone is moving forward together,
then success takes care of itself."
Henry Ford**

An effective team environment contributes to the organization in several ways. Perhaps one of the most important is through the role teams play in managing change. Most organizational processes impact many different people. Evaluating and identifying an existing process, or a new one, for its efficiency potential should include input from those involved. Using the team approach to change creates a venue for that input, and can lead to minimal resistance. In turn, that promotes more frequent process evaluations, allowing for perpetual fine-tuning of the organization.

Building Effective Teams

Create socially strong family unit

Delegate and trust

Hold accountable and follow up

Teach by example and principle

Be generous with appreciation

Set and maintain high standards

Building Team Trust—Team-building requires accountability at the top, the middle, the front line, right down to the employee levels. The key is to accomplish team building without demoralizing the individual.

Choosing Leaders Who Empower, Manage Change and Build Teams

One of the challenges to establishing and maintaining employee—participation programs is to provide clearly defined management and leadership roles. This needs to happen at all levels. Key ingredients to running successful programs are leadership, facilitation, and empowerment. Without clear, consistent definitions and guidelines, on which managers and leaders can base their style and actions, employee empowerment can become just an illusion, not a reality.

There are some effective tools for leadership development available on the market. They include the Multifactor Leadership Questionnaire, and Geert Hofstede's Value Survey Module. These instruments can help identify and develop effective leadership characteristics for you or the organization. Other methods include, 360 feedback programs, coaching, mentoring initiatives and well thought out succession planning.

Over the years and continuing today, leaders have been selected from the top down. The trend has been to select successful, task-oriented individuals. By placing them in leadership roles, the hope is that by example, their strengths will develop in those they lead.

Building Teams

But the very qualities that lead to success for the task-oriented person are those qualities that can inhibit their success at team leadership. They focus on the short-term task at hand, to the detriment of long-term thinking. They maintain control to improve their process, not recognizing any need to involve others or build alliances. Relying on consistency and order for their efficiency, they see open communication and consensus within a group as weaknesses. They perform their tasks best in the hierarchical style of management. They are comfortable with centralized power and control; with information, policies and procedures being dictated from the top.

This ingrained approach to management makes the task of establishing a team-oriented environment most challenging. Those in management positions resist sharing responsibility and control with their workers, missing the value of self-directed and empowered teams and individuals.

Changing a traditional organization to one that embraces the team environment requires leadership that believes in the value of the individual and the team; leadership that is prepared to devote the time and resources necessary both to build and maintain it. This is true at all levels of the organization. Then once that commitment is made, those in leadership positions must build teams of workers capable of taking an active role in developing the organization into a more efficient, competitive entity, able to change and grow to meet the demands of its industry.

Senior management considers effective leaders to be valued members who form work teams or groups that contribute to the organizational goals. To do this, leaders will need to be able to motivate and empower, and to establish trust at both the individual and group levels.

The first definition of motivate in the dictionary is "to provide with an incentive." Toward that end, the capable leader will seek to understand the individual, to know their needs and wants. Through this awareness, the leader can help the individual make the connection between reaching the team's and/or organization's goals, and thus, reaching their own.

With this connection made, the charge is to set high standards; challenging and encouraging everyone towards a level of performance and productivity beyond their expectations. In support of this, the individual team members can be coached and mentored, promoting innovation and nourishing creativity. As each member of the team is strengthened, so is the team.

Empowering

Competent leaders know the best way to create a solid organization is to empower subordinates. Give them a task, delegate the necessary authority, and let them do the work. Empowering the team does not mean omitting checks and making corrections when necessary.

When mistakes happen, leaders ensure followers sort out what happened and why. We all make mistakes, good conscientious leaders learn from mistakes. When mistakes are made Leaders step forward and see things from the other person' perspective, ask questions instead of giving condemnations, discusses his/her mistakes before criticizing and will seldom back people into a corner allowing the person to save face.

When mistakes are made Leaders step forward and see things from the other person' perspective, ask questions instead of giving condemnations, discusses his/her mistakes before criticizing and will seldom back people into a corner allowing the person to save face.

Mistakes are experience, "I know several thousand things that won't work"

Thomas Edison

Because people learn best by doing, leaders should be willing to take calculated risks and accept the possibility that less experienced subordinates will make mistakes. If subordinate leaders are to grow and develop trust, it is best to let them learn through experience. Good leaders allow space so followers can experiment within the bounds of intent-based tasks and plans.

On the opposite end of the spectrum, weak leaders who have not trained their followers sometimes insist, "They can't do it without me." Leaders who adopt this mentality are and being the center of the attention feel indispensable, their battle cry being, "I can't take a day off. I have to be here all the time. I must watch my followers' every move, or who knows what will happen?" are failed leaders, the fact is that no leader is irreplaceable. The organization will not stop functioning just because one leader, no matter how senior or central, steps aside.

The roles that empowerment and trust play in keeping everyone involved are critical. A leader engages his followers and gains their trust by conferring empowerment. This means sharing control of work tasks, and allowing everyone to participate in the decision-making process. As a team and its members gain momentum, their contributions must be acknowledged by allowing them to retain the power to effect change. Otherwise, the trust originally gained is broken and efforts to retain everyone's engagement in the process will be met with skepticism.

Another element of developing trust between a leader and the people is the leader's willingness to build and maintain communications in a way that is open and honest; sharing information, and avoiding at all costs, exploitation of a team and/or its members for the leader's own interests.

Organizations such as Southwest Airlines, Walt Disney Company, Google, and Wal-Mart value effective communications skills and as result have seen the value of a higher level of employee participation and have designed programs that encourage idea-sharing, bottom to top.

It is also easy to see why organizations and teams would flourish in such a participative environment, and to understand the benefit of empowering workers. Empowerment opens the organization or group to all the pooled talents and skills of the team. However, empowerment is not easy to establish because it is dependent upon the leaders psychology, values and attitudes.

Empowerment requires that a leader be secure in their own position, and not feel threatened by the loss of control implied by sharing it with others. (They would see it as a loss, rather than the gain that it is.) These leaders may represent as much as 90% of existing organizational leaders today.

Organizations moving forward will face the new challenges of emerging, competitive global markets, accelerated changes in technologies, less-predictable economic shifts, the increasing frequency of mergers and acquisitions, and a more rapidly changing workforce. To remain successful they will need to provide an environment that encourages everyone to participate in meeting the demands of change, and to create an integrated system of empowerment to achieve maximum benefit from all their people.

Leadership will be the key to breaking away from the more traditional, less flexible styles of management. An organization will need to have the kind of leadership that can imbed in its entire workforce the sense of a common strategic vision, and can encourage challenges to the status-quo. This is achieved through empowerment and knowledge sharing, resulting in heightened mutual trust in the process, the leadership, and the organization.

Teams are made up of Individuals

Once teams, empowerment, knowledge sharing and participation are understood, they can never be elevated above the needs of the individual. Maintaining individual consideration and helping to build the individuals self-esteem, should be the leader's first consideration. Treating all employees alike, as if one were no different from the other, is a tragic mistake. The leader who takes the time to build relationships with each of his or her workers will be in a position to better understand and evaluate each of their talents and abilities, some of which may not be seen otherwise.

It provides a more intimate knowledge of the workers' motivations, making the task of aligning the individual's vision with that of the organization more easily done. It also can give the leader a glimpse of the worker's shortcomings and failures, providing a base upon which to build a plan of remediation. And finally, giving the individual this kind of attention, accompanied by a greater exchange of information, achieves a higher level of trust and mutual respect.

Front-line leaders need to be able to stimulate followers' efforts to be creative and innovative by questioning their assumptions, and by getting them to approach old problems in new ways. By encouraging their workers to come up with and share new ideas and ways of tackling problems, a leader can help to facilitate the exchange of information, leading to a more involved and effective team of people.

Managing Change

A major function for leaders is to effectively drive and manage change, however research suggests that as much as 50% of all change initiatives fails to deliver expected results or meet intended objectives and that only one-third of organizational change initiatives are considered successful by organizational executives.

While there are many reasons why this failure occurs both at frontline level and organizational levels, it has been concluded that employees play a major role in the success or failure of change in their organizations.

The correlation is clear, leaders who cannot gain the commitment of the workers will find that their people are reluctant to commit their efforts and energy to change initiatives because they view it as intrusive and disruptive of the routines they are comfortable with and which will cause any meaningful social relationships to be shifted or altered. This reflects on their trust or lack of trust that they have with their boss, believing that the boss/leader will or will not consider their individual needs and is willing to provide them with support in radical changes in work loads, new work tasks and the painful process of building new work relationships.

Commitment from workers is gained by first, providing adequate resources to do the job. Second, providing positive encouragement and protecting workers against dysfunctional psychological stressors such as unnecessary criticism from the boss as well as from peers. Third, provide flexibility and respectful treatment regarding their personal needs. Fourth, provide ongoing training and development for the process and for the workers that benefits not only the organization but for their future careers and personal development. Finally, communicate everything all the time and make transparency the rule and expectation.

Creating this culture for change will tend to strengthen feelings of obligation and high levels of commitment. Employees will tend to reciprocate their personal treatment and consideration back to the organization and their boss building a trust relationship necessary for successful change engagement.

Organizational change succeeds when the leader can build a positive and healthy working environment where appreciation and individual consideration is openly exercised. The best leaders are able to establish a family-like organizational culture not only vertically up and down but genially horizontally across the team members themselves so that displays ongoing and continuous support for each member.

Chapter 4

Set the Example

A Leader Creates the Working Environment

Listens to my ideas

Treats me with respect

Values me as an individual

Patient—looks past my individual quirks

Gives me recognition and praise

Being Seen—Walking Around

The impression that a leader makes on others contributes to the success in leading them. How others perceive a leader depends on the leader's outward appearance, demeanor, actions, and words. Followers are constantly observing their leaders from the day they first arrive. Leaders at all levels who are willing to go everywhere, including where the conditions are the most severe, illustrate through their presence that they care. There is no greater inspiration than leaders who routinely share in team hardships and problems. Moving to where duties are performed allows the leader to have firsthand knowledge of the real conditions followers face. Followers who see or hear from the boss appreciate knowing that their unit has an important part to play.

Presence is not just a matter of the leader showing up; it involves the image that the leader projects. Presence is conveyed through actions, words, and the manner in which leaders carry themselves. A reputation is conveyed by the respect that others show, how they refer to the leader, and respond to the leader's guidance. Presence is a critical attribute that leaders need to understand. A leader's effectiveness is dramatically enhanced by understanding and developing the following areas:

Leadership Confidence

Personal bearing: Projecting a confident presence, a professional image of authority and caring.

Mental fitness: Having sound mental health and life balance, which sustain emotional health and conceptual abilities under prolonged stress.

Confidence: Projecting self-confidence and certainty in the organization's ability to succeed and able to demonstrate composure and outward calm through steady control over emotion.

Resilience: Showing a tendency to recover quickly from setbacks, failures, adversity, and stress while maintaining focus.

Leadership Confidence

Confidence is the faith that leaders place in their abilities to act properly in any situation, even under stress and with little information. Leaders who know their own capabilities and believe in themselves are confident. Self-confidence grows from professional competence. Too much confidence can be as detrimental as too little confidence. Both extremes impede learning and adaptability. Bluster—loudmouthed bragging or self-promotion—is not confidence. Truly confident leaders do not need to advertise their gift because their actions prove their abilities.

Confidence is important for leaders and teams. The confidence of a good leader is contagious and quickly permeates the entire organization, especially in dire situations. Confident leaders help followers control doubt while reducing team anxiety. Combined with strong will and self-discipline, confidence spurs leaders to do what must be done in circumstances where it would be easier to do nothing.

Flexibility

Resilient leaders can recover quickly from setbacks, shock, adversity, and stress while maintaining their focus. Their resilience rests on will, the inner drive that compels them to keep going, even when exhausted, hungry, afraid, cold, and wet. Flexible leaders allow organizations to meet challenging or demanding situations with results oriented actions and decisions that carry them to a fruitful conclusion.

Resilience and the will to succeed are not sufficient to carry the day during hard times. Competence and knowledge guide the energies of a strong will to pursue courses of action that lead to business success. The leader's premier task is to instill resilience and a team spirit in followers. That begins with effective and ongoing training and development.

Flexibility is essential when pursuing business efficiency, no matter what the working conditions are, a strong personal attitude helps prevail over any adverse external conditions. Followers will experience situations when it would seem easier to quit or reduce productivity rather than give true quality effort to a difficult task. During those times, everyone needs an inner source of energy to press on to completion. When things go badly, a leader must draw on inner reserves to gain the followers commitments and desire for quality.

Leaders are Environmental Creators—B = F (i.e.)

B = F (i,e) is a formula I use to remind me of how important leadership is and its impact on others and the group. Breaking down the formula shows the importance of how leadership behavior affects followers.

$$B = F\,(i,e)$$

Behavior (B) is a function (F) of the individual (i) and the environment (e).

As leaders our assumptions influence how we behave towards others and others will respond with the behavior we expect. A leader must be creative and value creativity in his/her followers. Leaders must be agents for creativity. Creativity allows organizations to be flexible, adaptive and reactive to change.

Good leaders know how to harness the collective creativity of the group. They know how to work with the followers in a way that encourages the open flow of ideas and communication in a positively-created, working environment.

Creating this type of environment cannot be done through intimidation and fear; it must be through patience and the act of instilling within the group, a desire to participate.

There is a direct correlation between a leader who has positive relations within his or her group and effective communications, which can't help but to positively impact performance within the follower, as well as within the organization. Positive relations will foster intellectual stimulation, and an aura of feeling comfortable enough to question processes and business practices. It will also promote employees to feel like they are included in on decision making and changes. Their value for thinking is acknowledged as a valuable contributor to the organization.

Leaders create an environment in which ideas can flourish and see the light of day. To do this, leaders must be self-confident and have faith in themselves and others. People in leadership positions need a solid sense of self. It serves them well in times of turmoil, which inevitably await those who aspire to lead. The way people feel about themselves affects virtually every aspect of their lives. Self-esteem, which emerges from a sense of confidence, thus becomes the key to success or failure. In effect, effective leaders defy the law of averages and win because they expect success from themselves.

Leaders Must Believe in the Organizations Cause

A critical aspect of a work environment is the leaders' actions toward his workers and the just cause of the organization. This sense of righteousness to the cause will also strengthen resolve. Conversely, where the leaders do not believe in the virtue of their actions, they will lack commitment and will be hindered by self-doubt. Such uncertainty will be apparent to others, undermining the confidence of the followers and encouraging their opponents. It will contribute to eventual defeat and failure.

It is important for each leader to become convinced of the worthiness of the mission, on some deeply felt level. Even when the immediate objective seems questionable, the leader must find justification in some indisputable value, such as support of the nation's honor. Then, that conviction must fortify all of the leader's actions. When a leader exudes a quiet confidence, surety, and decisiveness, followers will be inspired and opposition will be weakened.

Often times, effective leaders are described as "strong," "powerful," "magnetic," and "charismatic." But whatever else they may be, they certainly are self-confident. From this confidence, leaders are able to mobilize and inspire individuals and groups to make their own personal dreams and objectives come true. It is simply impossible for leaders to have this confidence if they truly cannot support the cause for which they are employed.

Leaders Encourage Creativity

Where only unquestioning obedience is valued, and where only strict adherence to rigid procedures is allowed, inflexibility and predictability are the consequences. It has led to the downfall of many organizations and small business enterprises. To succeed as a leader, or even to survive in a constantly changing and dangerous environment, creativity and adaptability are essential. This is where leaders must apply their foundational knowledge to the objective at hand and develop solutions; even in situations where there is no textbook answer.

Good Leaders are Good Followers

People everywhere are always looking for someone to follow or for someone to lead them. A leader is a person who goes ahead of others to direct or guide them or to show them how to do something. Leaders not only tell others what to do and how to do it, they also show them by example. Most importantly, leader's help others grow.

Employees look to their leader for direction as well as leadership. They listen to their words and observe their actions. Often workers will pattern how they treat others after the advice they are given, or they follow what they see a leader-type do.

Here are some questions to ask yourself:

1. What can I do as a leader that will help those who I have influence over?
2. How can I developing characteristics that will help me become a good leader as well as a good follower?
3. What are some ways you are, or can be a leader in your home? In your community?

Each of us is a leader. Nearly every person at some time, somewhere, in some way leads another person or group. Our lives touch the lives of others, and we influence them whether or not we intend to. Our influence, which is different from that of anyone else, is our leadership.

Since in one way or another nearly all of us are leaders, it is important that we learn to be good leaders. With good leadership skills, we can improve ourselves, help others, and strengthen our relationships with our friends and family members. As leaders, we can improve the organization and work harmoniously with other departments.

The value of good front-line leaders is that they help to create better line workers. Salesmen can sell more goods, managers can do better work, and the president or CEO's can make better decisions; inspire, train, supervise, motivate and do other important things that good leaders do.

We can develop the ability to lead if we will work at it. We need to prepare ourselves by learning the principles of good leadership through observing and studying the fundamentals, and then we must live these principles daily.

The model leader learns to follow perfectly. In order to become truly effective leaders, we must learn to listen, trust, build bridges, and follow. This requires that we learn to identify and follow good examples. We need to find leaders who:

Desired Leadership Characteristics

Study their trade and perfect it.

Serve others and put their own needs second

Have integrity and are honest

Are slow to anger

Are respected by others

Eager to teach others

Leaders Must Respect Their Followers; They Don't Have to Like Them

As strange as this may seem, leaders must have respect for those they lead but they don't have to like them. Disliking someone because of their personal lifestyle, poor manners or individual style, does not mean you have the right to shun, openly ignore, speak down, or insult them in a disrespectful manner. Respecting differences that you do not like requires characteristics that many leaders find hard to master.

Those characteristics include empathy, compassion and tolerance. Think about how many times your personal preferences had impact on how you treated those under your direction? The office worker who has multiple piercings, the gay worker, the red-neck tough guy; whatever the example, at one time or another we have let our prejudices show through our words or deeds, causing mistrust and caution. Putting misdirected personal opinions and biases aside is critical.

Respect is perhaps one of the more important qualities leaders can have, because it means they genuinely care for those they lead. If they respect those they lead, they want to help them improve their lives; they are concerned for their needs and want to help them reach their goals. At all times and in all ways in our leadership responsibilities, it is through our respect for the individual that we can help others accomplish this goal. Respect is a powerful motivator.

Leaders make sure that followers understand the purpose of their work. The leaders help them to understand their part in the work and to gain a vision of their important responsibilities. We need to give those who are to follow our leadership the vision we have of the purpose of our work, and help them understand the roles they are to play.

Leaders Inspire Others to Follow By Choice

Highly effective leaders understand the principle of agency or choice. They create eagerness in their followers; they do not use force or fear. When we attempt to force anyone to follow, we are using power and authority that define the organization and not us as individuals. Commitment becomes in apportion to the force we use. If we use a large amount of force and intimidation we receive very little commitment and trust. If we are to lead in an effective, committed manner, we must allow others the freedom to choose.

Effective leaders let people know what is expected of them. It calls for honesty; we must let others know what we expect from them, and what they can expect from us. When we give them responsibilities, we must carefully explain their duties, the time involved, the meetings they are to attend, and what they must accomplish. It has been my experience that when people head in the wrong direction, it is because they did not have a clear understanding of what was expected of them.

Motivational Considerations

Meaningful and worthwhile tasks help people feel needed. Asking people to do things simply to keep them busy usually does not accomplish good results. As leaders, we need to help our followers feel that what they do is worthwhile. When we lead, we must be certain that we do not infringe on the time of others by giving them tasks that are not necessary.

Often times when leaders do not delegate to their people, it is because they simply do not understand they have to be responsible both to the organizational purpose and to the people. Too often leaders are afraid to risk poor results or make mistakes so they tend to hold on to responsibility or micro-manage their people. Workers who are micromanaged and have little control over the work they perform describe the work environment as stressful, the boss as overbearing and report a diminished sense of self-worth.

Leadership has an element of responsibility to help the people grow, not only to build the organization, but also to build and expand the workers and other emerging leaders. This should be a leaders purpose—to help our followers grow and gain experiences and success. This usually cannot be achieved with a micro-management style. Growth will occur in an environment in which workers are trusted to carry out their jobs in ways they feel important and allow them the autonomy to make decisions.

Leaders do the Unexpected

An indispensable ingredient of a leader's success is an almost tangible self-confidence, which causes them to radiate certainty, composure, and authority, and breathe life into an otherwise dull situation. This also includes not being afraid to do unexpected, uncalculated acts on behalf of those who he/she influences. Through his aura of conviction, he also inspired people who in many cases had already resigned themselves to execution, to join in his actions and save themselves and others.

Effective Leaders Respect and Value the Individual

One historical example of this component is reflected in the life actions of Abraham Lincoln confronting General Grant, and Secretary of War Stanton, before the end of the Civil War.

Leaders Do the Unexpected

General Grant and Secretary of War Stanton were bitterly criticizing Lincoln for his leniency that they believed was destroying the discipline of the army; they stated publicly that his disregard for disciplinary guidelines would ruin him politically; Lincoln seldom let the critics get to him when making difficult decisions.

For instance, one incident occurred that so embittered the military and most northern citizens at the time, but is now viewed as a true act of compassion for the individual.

A soldier's mother visited with Lincoln pleading with Lincoln to spare her condemned son from the firing squad; her son was caught trying to make his way home. He was caught, court-martialed for desertion and sentenced to be shot. The widowed mother explained to Lincoln that she had already lost her husband and three sons to the war, and this son was the last.

Lincoln listened quietly and then produced a piece of paper instructing the boy to be released immediately to his mother.

The generals were appalled when they learned that Lincoln not only pardoned the widow's son, but also publicly declared, "I am unwilling for any boy under eighteen to be shot." Then, turning to his Secretary of War Stanton, Lincoln added, "I have never been sure but what I might drop my gun and run myself, if I were in battle. Anyway, I don't see that shooting will do him any good."

Lincoln had no hidden agenda, he spoke from his heart, he was not afraid to do the unexpected; he did what others were afraid to do because of fear of losing their power and positions. Lincoln led the public and nation in the direction he truly felt was best for them. As a result, he was admired by most and despised by others. His promises were kept, his integrity was never compromised, and leaders after him have seldom matched his humility.

> **"If you are the leader, your people expect you to create their future. They look into your eyes, and they expect to see strength and vision. To be successful, you must inspire and motivate those who are following you. When they look into your eyes, they must see that you are with them."**
>
> *Lee Iacocca*

Leaders Set the Example

Leaders play a critical part when it comes to maintaining focus on the purpose of the business and not on plans and paper jargon. They are at the forefront of adapting to changes in the business environment and exploiting emerging opportunities by applying a combination of intuition, analytical problem solving, systems integration, and leadership by example—as close to the front line employees as feasible.

To see and feel the situation at hand and exert leadership by personal presence and example, front line leaders position themselves as closely as possible to the production or manufacturing with all necessary means to maintain contact with upper management.

Proximity to production provides today's organizational leaders with the required awareness to apply quick creative thinking in collaboration with all level of leadership. It facilitates adjustments for deficiencies in production planning and shortens reaction time when applying sound operating solutions to changing real time events. In some areas of organizations creative leadership is instrumental in achieving swift transitions to customer demands or engineering upgrades. Transition efforts require creating ad-hoc teams, integrating new equipment and technologies, as well as adjusting customer or market conditions.

Leaders Shoulder the Weight and Responsibility

> In Saudi Arabia, I had the opportunity to travel and visit some of the ancient engineering marvels of the Dedanite kingdom at Al Ula and became interested in ancient ruins.
>
> There is a fascination with some ruins that have heavy weights on top of columns and cut stone; some hold all the weight while others have fallen and crumbled.
>
> Those that remain standing tend to stand because, over time, they have had to bear the majority of the weight on top. I feel that strong leaders have similar characteristics.
>
> They are committed and they are not afraid to share the weight with others, but we must first be willing to have the entire weight on our shoulder. The leader cannot ask of others what his is not willing to do himself.

As a leader, your every action is watched, picked apart, and judged. In essence, your head is always above the crowd. The greatest inspirations have come from leaders who set the proper example. They practice what they preach and ask nothing more of their followers than that which they require of themselves.

As an infantry platoon leader in Korea, I was assigned to duty on the DMZ, with very little leadership experience. Being forward deployed on the border, our soldiers had to be in top physical condition. Each day, the platoon would start the day at four o'clock in the morning with a three mile run. Each week ended with a twelve mile road march up a steep, Korean mountain dubbed, "Misery Hill."

When I first arrived and took over the platoon, the morale of the thirty-two soldiers was one of complaining, criticizing and poor performance. During the runs, no one was calling cadence or chanting the traditional Army cadence calls used to help keep the soldiers minds off of the discomfort of the runs.

Things were not much better during the weekly road marches up Old Misery. There was no interaction between leaders. During periodical stops, everyone, including the leaders, found their own plots of ground and either sat down or laid down. The only interaction between soldier and leader was when our Company Commander happened by and shouted out insults and threats to everyone. His presence brought fear to all who encountered his tirades and ranting.

One evening I was sitting outside our assembly area, thinking of what I could do. I asked a trusted NCO, Sergeant Evans, what he would do about the problem. His observation was straight forward and to the point.

"Sir, no one is leading. Sir, you need to set the example."

Kindly stated, he said—Take charge. No one was setting the example. I learned a valuable lesson:

Doing nothing is not leadership

I immediately acted. Each morning for the next month, I led the run, calling cadence and leading the chants as we ran. I then challenged all my platoon sergeant and squad leaders to prepare themselves to take turns leading the runs. In order to help prepare them, I decided that the platoon sergeant and all the squad leaders would participate in evening two mile runs without the troops, taking turns practicing different cadences and songs. We did this for several weeks. The results were amazing. Our runs became faster, the morale was high, and we had no one fall out or lag behind. The big difference was that we as the leadership group—were a team.

My second goal was to improve our road march performance. When I arrived, it was common to have at least seven to ten soldiers fall out and be picked up by the ever present, First Sergeants jeep. I noticed that during critical breaks, the leadership was sitting around taking care of their own sore feet or just relaxing.

Stay in Touch and Visible

I knew that the front-line leaders were the key to motivating the soldiers.

During long movements, I began a routine during brief breaks of asking and requesting selected soldiers two things each time we stopped. First, how were they doing on water and how were their feet doing? Second, I had them take their socks off so I could see the condition of their feet.

I would try and visit the ones who were really struggling and speak some words of advice and encouragement. No yelling, no criticism or condemning.

The action had its intended results; I began to notice that the squad leaders began to check on their members at each stop and had them take their socks off, inspecting sore feet and suggesting ways to keep them free of blisters.

The power of example clearly had an impact resulting in improved performance, morale, and reduced injuries. Perhaps more importantly, it extended to the soldiers what they really wanted most, someone who really cared. Afterwards, there were no stragglers, no fallouts; everyone finished contributing to the success of the platoon.

A leader is a person who goes ahead of others to direct or guide them or to show them how to do something. Leaders not only tell others what to do and how to do it, they also show them by example. As leaders we must be willing to go further, carry a little more of the load, be willing to give the last cup of water to another, but we must always cross the line first and lead the way.

"First they came . . ." is a popular poem attributed to Martin Niemöller describing how Hitler during his rise to power purged group after group without much opposition.

First they came for the communists, and I did not speak out—because I was not a communist;

Then they came for the socialists, and I did not speak out—because I was not a socialist;

Then they came for the trade unionists, and I did not speak out—because I was not a trade unionist;

Then they came for the Jews, and I did not speak out—because I was not a Jew;

Then they came for me—and there was no one left to speak out for me.

Chapter 5

Communication

> It is the leader's job to create an environment of honest and open communications, to create an environment in which followers discuss mistakes and learn from them. I don't want people hiding or distorting the truth for fear of reprisal.

Ensuring Shared Understanding

Organizational leaders know themselves, the mission, and the message. They owe it to their organization and their subordinates to share as much information as possible. An open, two-way exchange of information reinforces sharing team values and signals constructive input is appreciated. Communicating openly and clearly with superiors is important but critically important for organizational leaders. Understanding the superior's intent, priorities, and thought processes makes it easier to anticipate future planning and resource priorities. Understanding the azimuth of the higher headquarters reduces the amount of course corrections at the lower levels, thus minimizing friction and maintaining a stable organizational climate.

Using Persuasion to Build Teams and Consensus

Persuasion is an important method of communications. Well-developed skills of persuasion and openness to working through controversy in a positive way help to overcome resistance and build support. These characteristics are important in dealing with other organizational leaders, multinational partners, and in the inter-departmental arena. By reducing grounds for misunderstanding, persuasion reduces wasted time in overcoming unimportant issues. It also ensures involvement of others, opens communication with them, and places value on their opinions—all critical team-building actions. Openness to discussing one's position and a positive attitude toward a dissenting view often defuses tension and saves time. By demonstrating these traits, leaders also provide an example that subordinates can use in self-development.

In some circumstances, persuasion may be inappropriate. At work, all leaders must often make decisions quickly, requiring a more direct style when leading and deciding on courses of action.

Impact of Communications

Every employee focus group, 360-degree feedback session, opinion survey, and personal interview I have conducted over the years, identify one common problem within the workings of an organization—poor communication.

Effective leaders understand the holistic picture of communications and its impact on the organization. Communication is not a cold impersonal process; it requires a deep interpersonal connection with the people around. It requires acceptance of multi-sources; the follower, the customer, the superiors, and colleague. It requires a truly 360-degree assessment.

The real problem in business is that many leaders see communication as unnecessary, too time consuming, or they are just not good at it. That's because sometimes making decisions without communicating is easier to do.

What we need to understand, is that effective leaders who communicate well, do it in tones of support rather than loudness. They intend to be helpful rather than hurtful. They tend to use communication to bind workers together rather than to drive them apart. They tend to build rather than to belittle.

Balanced Communication

Leaders use effective communications which are expressions of affection and not anger, facts and not fabrication, compassion and not contention, respect and not ridicule, counsel and not criticism, correction and not condemnation. Their words are spoken with clarity and not with confusion. They may be tender or they may be tough, but they must always be tempered.

Another challenge that leaders face in the workforce is to condition ourselves away from the cold, calculating, business mindset, towards developing feelings for our followers and understanding that we are dealing with people of responsibility and character; mothers, fathers, sisters and brothers. When we develop this concern for the condition of others, we then will communicate with them in a way they listen and feel appreciated. We will then, as good leaders, win their trust and commitment.

The right type of communication helps us to develop respectful relationships and ultimately build up our organizations, also building up those whom we lead.

Providing Clear Direction

Communicate how to accomplish a task or skill

Followers expect challenging tasks, quality training, and adequate resources.

They should be given appropriate freedom of action.

Providing clear direction allows followers the freedom to modify plans and assignments to adapt to changing circumstances.

Directing while adapting to change is a continuous process.

For example, a line supervisor always takes the time and has the patience to explain to the followers what is required of them. The supervisor does it by calling them together for a few minutes to talk about the workload and the time constraints. Although many followers will tire of hearing from the supervisor about how well they are doing and that they are essential to operations accomplishment, they know it is true and appreciate the comments. Every time the supervisor passes information during a meeting, he sends a clear signal: people are cared for and valued. The payoff ultimately comes when there arise problems and as events unfold, the supervisor will not have time to explain, acknowledge performance, or motivate them. Followers will do their jobs because their leader has earned their trust.

Seven effective communications principles that employees say they desire:

Listen to my ideas and what I say

Don't make unreasonable demands.

Communicate with us.

Encourage participation.

Show genuine concern for our issues.

Don't do only what he or she, the leader, wants.

Be sensitive to problems and needs at work

Hearing is not the same as Listening Someone

During my first week as Assistant Professor at Penn State University, I met with the president of the school who asked me how I was going to teach all the materials I had been given.

I replied, "I will teach in such a way that everyone will understand and no one will misunderstand."

He then asked me, "How do you plan to do that? I can't think of any tenured professor who has managed to accomplish what you're saying."

I really had not expected that response. I thought for a moment and replied, "Well, I plan to speak the truth, choose words that are easy to understand, avoid arguments, avoid offending, speak as kindly as I can and I plan to listen and hear what they say."

To my delight he said, "You may have a chance here. Not too many of my professors know how to hear by being good at listening."

"Hearing is *not* the same as Listening. Leaders need to listen *and* feel what is being said."

Leaders must learn to become good listeners. Leaders create an atmosphere of understanding and acceptance that makes people comfortable, because they listen with a patient ear and take the time to listen to and understand their people's needs, thus demonstrating true concern.

A different but effective way to listen to people is to let people think through their own ideas by asking them questions. This helps them understand what points need to be made. To be good leaders, we must help people solve their own problems and meet their own challenges. We can ask them questions to help them consider possibilities for resolving problems and guide them through the process.

"No Excuses" Leadership

We have too many leaders today who coin the phrase; I don't want "no excuses"; which I have never understood. Making such a dead-end statement cuts short any communication that might prove useful to both parties. Too many leaders do not realize the damage they do with their form and style of communication. They see condemnation and tough talk as a sign of power and strength. These leaders as well as all leadership must recognize the power of positive, effective communication and practice it daily. By applying good communication skills, we become better leaders and find greater success. Our communications are at the core of our relationships with others. If we are to expect commitment, performance and trust, we must develop trusting relationships with our employees.

Our communication reflects in our integrity and ability to be trusted. Therefore, we must be careful not only *what* we communicate, but also *how* we do so. People can be strengthened or shattered by the message and the manner in which we communicate.

We must express confidence in others and motivate them to find solutions and make decisions. New, emerging leaders within the organization often times find it very difficult to make good decisions all the time by themselves, but are not inclined to ask for help because they do not want to be seen or perceived as incapable. Leaders can find courage and strength in the help of others.

Avoid Destructive Communication

There are certain kinds of communication which destroy relationships and are not for our development but rather, our destruction. They result in diminished, opportunity motivation. One of the major ways to destroy a department or division is for front-line leaders to participate in, or allow the use of gossip, rumor, and slander.

Perhaps the four most common destructive forms of communication are those of lying, blaming, criticizing, and anger. Leaders not only stop this type of communication, but they must set the example and not engage in it.

Lying

The first of these forms of negative communication is that of lying. To lie is to be untruthful, deceptive, deceitful, and dishonest. This is a basic communication problem which is not new; but always has the same results. It will destroy a leader's integrity and trust. Integrity is the core of our character. Without integrity we have a weak foundation upon which to build other leadership characteristics.

Blaming

A second destructive form of communication is that of blaming. This is a condemning communication. It is interesting that when people are afraid to accept accountability, they begin to place the blame on others. It has been my experience that weak leaders tend to blame mistakes and problems on others or on certain circumstances. When we attempt to place responsibility for our choices on others, we are responding in a leaderless manner. More importantly, do not allow those under you to fall into the habit of blaming, encourage them to seek root causes—never blame or finger pointing.

Criticizing

A third destructive form of communication is that of criticizing. Positive or constructive criticism is feedback given with the purpose of helping another person to grow and to develop. This is both helpful and needful and is generally accepted and appreciated.

Negative criticism is intended to hurt and often to defame and to destroy. This caustic communication is cruel, and it tends to crush the character of all of those about whom it is directed.

Anger

A fourth form is anger. This is perhaps the most common form of destructive communication. Anger causes anguish to everyone who experiences the feeling, as well as to those who are the recipients of this emotional explosion. I have an expression I have used in my family when angry words are exchanged or tempers flare, "the sprit has been sucked out of this home." This term describes bad feelings and a breakdown of communication that destroys any enthusiasm or eagerness.

Anger shows a lack of self-control and an inability to relate in a professional way to others. It is a senseless substitute for self-control. It is sometimes used as a selfish strategy to gain control of a relationship.

> **The moment a leader becomes angry they show a great weakness.**

Effective leaders view communications as a tool intended to be helpful rather than hurtful. Communications can bind us together rather than drive us apart and it can build our employees rather than belittle them.

Leaders never Criticize, Condemn, nor Complain

I am convinced that most front line leaders do not understand the principles about personal criticism, especially the criticism of their followers. I do not refer to the kind of criticism the dictionary defines as "the act of passing judgment as to the merits of anything." (*Random House Dictionary*, unabridged ed., s.v. "criticism.")

That kind of criticism is inherent in our freedom of speech and seeking truths. In the political world, critical evaluation inevitably accompanies any knowledgeable exercise of the cherished freedoms of speech and of the press. In the private world, we have a right to expect critical evaluation of anything that is put into the marketplace or the public domain. Sports writers, reviewers of books and music, scholars, investment analysts, and those who test products and services must be free to exercise their critical faculties and to inform the public accordingly. This kind of criticism is usually directed toward issues, and it is usually constructive.

The criticism that leaders must avoid is the act of passing severe judgment; censure; faultfinding. Faultfinding is the act of pointing out faults, especially faults of a petty nature. It is related to "backbiting," which is attacking the character or reputation of a team member. This kind of criticism is generally directed toward a person or persons, and it is generally destructive in nature.

We are all prone to see the limitations and the weaknesses of our employees and our boss's, yet there are leaders who find fault and always criticize in a destructive way.

There is a difference in criticism. If we can criticize constructively for the true purpose of helping better the person or the situation, we may change beneficially and properly some of the things that are being done. But if our purpose is for faultfinding, of pointing out the weaknesses and failings of others in a destructive manner, our leadership will be dismissed and rejected by those who follow us, making our efforts futile. It can be one of the most un-motivating experiences.

I am not suggesting that leaders not be critical. Growth comes of correction, strength comes of change, and effective leaders are those who can acknowledge mistakes pointed out by others and knowledgably change their course.

What I am suggesting is that leaders turn from the negativism that so permeates our workplace, and look for the remarkable talent among those with whom we associate. That we speak of our employee's strengths more than we speak of their faults.

I have often heard department managers say, "I'm speaking my mind and telling you the truth."

The fact that something is true is not always a justification for communicating it. I maintain that a man who speaks his mind has poor judgment, specifically, there is "a time to speak," and there is also "a time to keep silence." Effective leaders know how to apply this principle.

As a leader, truth exists as an absolute, but our *use* of truth should be disciplined by other values. For example, it is wrong to make statements with the intent of harm or to gain advantage, even if the statements are true. It is wrong to threaten to reveal embarrassing facts unless a favor is done, even if the facts are true. We call that a crime of blackmail. Doctors, lawyers, and other professionals are forbidden to reveal facts they have received in confidence, even though those facts are true.

Truth is powerful and absolute in its existence, but its communication should usually be guided by companion principles. Leaders who use the sword of truth, might not be used to build their followers, but might be misused of truth, might not use it to build their followers, but might use it carelessly to embarrass, debase, or deceive others. The sign of an effective leadership is often *silence*. Some truths are best left unsaid. There is not a better sign of good leadership than the leader who allows an employee to save face and move on.

A leader, who focuses on faults though they may be true, tears down those under him. The virtues of patience, kindness, mutual respect, and loyalty, all rest to some degree on the principle that even though something is true, we are not necessarily justified in communicating it to any and all persons at any and all times.

The use of truth should also be constrained by the principle of unity and team work. A leader, who focuses on faults, fosters dissensions and divisions among fellow members, splinters any hope of real, team participation and the establishment of trust.

Avoiding destructive personal criticism does not mean that leaders need to be docile or indifferent to defective policies, deficient practices, or wrongful conduct in the organization. Leaders should not avoid constructive criticism of such conditions. The leader should avoid personal attacks and shrill denunciations. Our public communications—even those protesting against deficiencies—should be reasoned in content and motivating.

Don't Slap the Dolphin

When I lived in Orlando Florida, my best friend was a trainer at Sea World and invited me to watch one of his training sessions. The day came and my friend began his training session with the dolphin's swimming the perimeter of the pool then performing small jumps and finally spectacular aerial acrobats and twirls. The discipline was unbelievable and the skills these animal's possessed was spectacular. I learned that it cost nearly half a million dollars to properly train one dolphin and what they learned was for life as long as they were properly trained and nourished with the right foods.

At the end of the training session, my friend invited me to take a tour of the holding pins and veterinarian facilities. During the tour, I noticed a medium sized pin with a dolphin alone, by himself. I asked my friend why he was separated from the others. He explained that this particular dolphin was being prepared to be released back into the ocean the following day because he could no longer perform.

Several weeks earlier, a group of college interns were learning how to train dolphins; part of the training was behavior conditioning through rewarding proper behavior with rewards such as fish and squid. The process requires a trainer to either throw the fish into the dolphin's mouth or let it fall into the mouth just before the dolphin reaches the trainers hand. During the process of feeding the dolphins in this manner, one of the interns held onto the fish too long and the dolphin delivered a painful bite the intern's hand, leaving a nasty cut. Without giving it much thought, the intern reached down and as the happy, chattering dolphin appeared for another tasty morsel, the intern delivered a hard slap to the dolphin on its head.

When a dolphin becomes offended or attacked by the one he has trust in, that dolphin will never perform again and will go to the bottom of the pool, surfacing only to get air but will never perform again.

On my way home, I thought about the dolphin that had been slapped and refused to perform again. I couldn't help but compare it to how people react with criticism and mental slaps, very few people really perform afterwards. I learned a valuable lesson—Don't Slap the Dolphin.

Leaders Should Look for the Admirable Qualities in Their People

When leaders look for the admirable qualities in their people, they are better able to prevent difficulties. They are also able to work together to resolve difficulties that arise, communication becomes welcomed and revered, and constructive advice is accepted and barriers are lowered.

Seek Out the Better Qualities

While working with a processing plant in Arkansas, the plant manager came to me to express grievances against his night superintendent. He was very critical of the supervisor and lashed out at his poor performance and attitude, which was getting worse.

After several minutes of listening to the manager criticizing him, I asked, "What qualities did you see in him when he was hired, if you consider him so incompetent and reckless now?"

The plant manager thought for a moment and said, "Well, I suppose he had some good qualities, but I can't remember any. He must have changed."

I suggested that he take some time to cool off and try to remember the characteristics he had once admired in this superintendent. In a few weeks I asked him how the superintendent was doing. With a sense of excitement he stated that he had remembered some of the superintendent's admirable qualities. Before, he had been so consumed with seeing his faults that he had failed to see his good qualities.

Leaders, learn to listen, and listen to learn from your people. Taking time to listen is essential in keeping the lines of communication intact. If people are an important asset to your department or organization, they deserve prime time! Yet less important agendas and projects are given priority, leaving only leftover moments for listening to your people.

Conducting regular meetings to discuss problems openly and calmly, at all levels, are essential to knowing your people. Discussions should be conducted in a respectful way, without loud arguments or contention. The best organizations I have been part of had one common thread; they held daily/regular department meetings and monthly plant/organization meetings.

While serving with a management team in Waco Texas, our team, under the leadership of Ray Parma, seldom had trouble, because there were hardly ever raised voices and arguments in our weekly meetings, Ray insisted that our communication be respectful, and as result, there developed a genuine respect and working relationships among the members. It is only when we raised our voices that the sparks flew and tiny molehills become great mountains of contention. When those few times happened, Ray quickly stepped in and did not allow it to build for very long.

Communicate in positive ways

> **"In what ways do expressions of appreciate in and recognition influence a relationship between leader and follower?"**

I have asked the question "In what ways do expressions of appreciate in and recognition influences a relationship between leader and follower?"

Impact that sincere appreciation has on workers

I am more committed

I want to do well

Improves communications within our group

I enjoy coming to work

I feel motivated

If you ask most work groups. "How does negative communication from me—such as criticism, and fault-finding—affect our relationship?" You will be told:

Generally I am painfully aware of my weaknesses, and I don't need frequent reminders from you.

I have never changed for the better as a result of constant criticism and condemnations.

What my boss offers as constructive criticism is actually destructive.

What kind of results do you expect from constant complaints or criticism?

I hate when my boss compares my weaknesses to the strengths of others.

Case of Negative Communications

Pat Boyer was the owner of a meat processing company in Colorado, by his own admission he was "intense"; a word that he liked to use to label himself, perhaps because he felt that strong leaders had to be intense with people.

During a daily meeting, he was reviewing production data and personnel issues and started to ask questions of the group. The purchasing manager was hesitant in giving answers, only because while he knew things were fine, he did not want to say something that was a bit off; he knew the owner was an intense man.

After the meeting, the owner pulled the production manager aside and asked, "You seemed a little uncertain in there, what's going on." His tone was condescending and negative, his body language showed signs of disgust and anger.

The owner's intensity was actually negative communication which had a devastating effect on those around him. There

> were few who felt they could be honest and candid, essentially denying the president of much needed information and insight. While the owner saw intensity as positive leadership characteristic, it literally shut people down.

This is not a major example of an explosive boss, but it is a common example of how leaders can create a fearful communication style and never really understand how it impacts those around them.

This particular leader honestly felt that his style was effective, in fact he would label it as intense, pushing hard, and directing, in reality he was shredding people's self-esteem and destroying their trust and respect for him as a leader.

Learn to Give Honest and Sincere Praise

> "A kick in the pants is just a few inches from a pat on the back—yet the results are miles apart"

People crave sincere appreciation; it is a reoccurring theme wherever I go when I ask employees, teachers and leaders themselves, what motivates them. As leaders we can focus on what employees do well, or what they do badly. I would suggest trying to focus on the good things those around you do, and let them know.

Giving praise is not a weakness nor will it make people soft. It is high on the motivation list. Let me list a few ways to deliver praise.

First, praise must be genuine and factual. It must be presented then followed up by an example. "Mary, I appreciate your hard work. The report you turned in helped the plant manager better understand our position in the market." Or "John, I appreciate you working on the ground beef grinder, you know it cost us a hundred-dollars-a-minute when it's down, you've saved us a lot of money."

This also goes for behavior. I have told employees who have made mistakes things such as, "I am glad you admitted the problem, it took courage to do that," and, "I admire how you handle difficult customers, it makes a difference when you are firm yet understanding."

Secondly, follow a compliment with a question such as, "The yield on your machines was great this month, how do you keep them running efficiently?" Putting a question on the end allows people to explain their skills and talents not simply leaving them not knowing how to respond.

Another good idea is to personalize the praise using their name. It demonstrates that you know them, and gives people a sense of importance that has a bonding effect.

Finally, give praise when the person isn't immediately around; such as during meetings, group sessions or to their immediate supervisors. Praise that is passed on to the individual has a powerful, self-worth affect. Giving praise tends to drive out fear from a group and creates an atmosphere of eagerness and gratitude.

> **Everyone likes a complement—Abraham Lincoln 1865**

Chapter 6

Trust and Respect

Effective Leaders are Respected and Trusted

Leaders have to learn that the interest of their people is their own interest, or they will never build effective teams in today's organizations. Truly effective leaders are trusted and respected by the people they lead, they are admired for their honesty, concern and personalized attention to them. However, it is not given easily; it has to be earned by the leader through example and "walking the talk".

Trust building begins with the individual; building relationships will lead to workers who try harder, volunteer readily and eventually become committed to the organization.

Three factors to building the foundation for trust

Ability

Integrity

Benevolence

These are the main factors that contribute to trust building. Trust is the willingness of our employees or those associated with us, to take risk, and the level of trust is an indication of the amount of risk that they are willing to take. It can be stated another way—Trust can be defined as a willingness to be vulnerable to their leader and is formed by the three factors of ability, integrity and benevolence.

Ability is the degree to which, we as leaders follow through on what we say, what we do and how it is done. It is the quality of our efforts compare to results we achieve. If we tell people one thing, even with good intentions, but do not have the authority or power to carry it out, then our ability is questioned and becomes degraded.

Integrity is who we are and how we are viewed by those around us based upon our history and interpersonal exchanges. It defines us to others. "If he says he will do it, he will," "be careful, he has a gambling problem," it is our ethics and values as seen by others and is the fabric of which we are made of.

There are so many disappointing breaches of integrity in leadership that has become too casual. A simple example is that of Governor Mark Sanford as reported by the AP national press in 2007 as follows:

"South Carolina Gov. Mark Sanford used state aircraft for personal and political trips, often bringing along his wife and children—contrary to state law regarding official use, an Associated Press investigation has found.

Records reviewed by the AP show that since he took office in 2003, the two-term Republican has taken trips on state aircraft to locations of his children's sporting events, hair and dentist appointments, political party gatherings and a birthday party for a campaign donor.

On March 10, 2006, a state plane was sent to pick up Sanford in Myrtle Beach and return him to Columbia, the state capital, at a cost of $1,265—when his calendar showed his only appointment in Columbia was "personal time" at his favourite discount hair salon. He had flown to Myrtle Beach on a private plane and attended a county GOP event.

Also, on five of the last six Thanksgiving weekends, Sanford used a state plane to fly himself, his wife and their four sons from the family's plantation in Beaufort County to Columbia for the state Christmas tree lighting. The cost for those flights alone: $5,536, including $2,869 for flying the plane empty to pick them up.

Sanford, 49, has been under increased scrutiny since he admitted in June to having a mistress in Argentina. He's vowed to stay in office and says he is trying to reconcile with his wife, though she moved out of the governor's official residence on Friday with their sons and plans to spend the school year at the family's beach house.

Last month, the AP revealed how Sanford had flown first class and business class on commercial airlines at taxpayer expense, despite a law requiring lowest-cost travel. On many occasions, records show, the governor mingled his non-official travels with official business." As reported by AP.

Leaders must maintain higher levels of integrity than those above and below his or her position; it is expected and demanded.

Benevolence is the extent to which we are believed to want to do good for others interests. It is our degree of goodness within us to share and to help others. A good leader demonstrates that he or she considers their people's needs above and beyond their own. The leader represents their people's needs to higher authorities effectively, and does not let his or her own ambition interfere with what is best for them; even if it risks the leaders own interests. It requires the leader to demonstrate consistent application of ethics and principle.

> **Benevolent leaders are willing to give more to others than they receive**

An element of benevolence is the ability to be kind. Kindness is the essence of greatness and the fundamental characteristic of leadership. Kindness is a passport that opens doors and fashions friends. It bonds people and molds relationships that are important to the workforce. The things that are important to us and ones that we remember most are the small acts of kindness that have been extended to us.

Kindness

> The power of kindness and its impact on people reminds me of a time when I was living in Saudi Arabia. My driveway was lined by shaggy trees that needed sheering that I had put off for a long time. One weekend a good friend of mine dropped by unannounced with all the tools to trim and shape the trees. We had a great time that weekend.
>
> This unexpected, unannounced act of kindness was appreciated and will stick in my memories as one act of kindness that can never be fully repaid.

The power of kindness should not be limited to outside our work; there is great power in benevolence that can benefit our workers. The attributes of thoughtfulness and kindness are inseparably linked with the principle of benevolence and trust building, kindness is the essence of an effective leader. Kindness should permeate all of our words and actions at work, there is no substitute for kindness at work, it is simply how a person treats others and we are the example, if we fail to set the example it may not happen within our teams.

As a leader, the things you say, the tone of your voice, the anger or calm of your words—these things are noticed by your workers. They see and learn both the kind and the unkind things we say or do. Nothing exposes our true selves more than how we treat one another in the workplace and people are more likely to trust a leader if they know he is compassionate and forgiving.

I have always attended the private funerals of those who I have been associated with at all levels, whether it was a son killed in an auto accident or a grandmother who passed of old age, I made it a point to be present. I have always visited workers and their families in the hospitals to say a few encouraging words. This generous visible display of compassion and caring has always without failure, inspired trust, loyalty and admiration from those around me.

It is unwise for a boss/leader to be casual regarding criticism or being critical of others openly as by habit. It gets in their blood, I suppose, and it becomes so natural they often don't even think about it. They seem to criticize everyone—the way the secretary makes calls, how an associate needs time off to take care of family issues and more.

Even when we think we are doing no harm by our critical remarks, consequences often follow.

> I am reminded of a boy who handed an envelope with twenty dollars to his father's boss at a company fund raising event, and told the boss it was for him. The boss told the boy to give the money to his secretary who would forward the funds to the organization's designated charity, he explained to the boy that he should mark on the envelope what organization the money was intended for. The boy hesitated for a moment, and then insisted the money was for the boss himself. When the boss asked why, the boy replied, "Because my father says you're one of the poorest bosses he ever had."

Lesson learned is that criticism has unseen impact on others in ways that are not immediately seen but has a powerful influence on perceptions and relationships.

One way you can measure your value as a leader is to ask, "How well am I doing in helping others reach their potential? Do I support others in the organization, or do I criticize them?" If you are criticizing others, you are weakening the organization. If you are building others, you are building the organization or department.

Importance of Trust

Leaders not only trust their followers but are trusted by them as well. They are not afraid to share responsibilities or teach them higher skills that require delegating and empowering others, giving them important things to do for their development. These leaders do not feel that they have to do it personally in order to get it done right; they are eager to share responsibility as a teaching opportunity for their followers benefit and growth.

> **An effective leader sees followers not for what they are now, but for what they can become.**

I have witnessed excellent, young, managers and workers walk away from organizations because they did not have meaningful work and were seen as too inexperienced to handle the job by their boss.

Violating Trust

While trust violations have been extensively studied under controlled laboratory conditions, these laboratory simulations are limited in the type of violations that it is possible to study and the repertoire of possible repair actions available. Studying actual trust violations in the workplace can expand our horizons. A recent study conducted a series of interviews and focus groups with members of organizational work groups to determine which factors most frequently contributed to breakdowns in trust.

Eight causes why leaders cannot gain workers trust:

1. Disrespectful behaviors: Discounting people or their contributions, disregarding feelings and input, and blaming other people for problems.
2. Communication issues: Not listening to others, not working to understand the other party, and breakdown in communication around major changes;
3. Unmet expectations: Broken promises, breaches in the psychological contract, breach of confidentiality, and breach of rules.
4. Ineffective leadership: Punishing those who challenged authority, poor decisions, favoritism, or unwillingness to address major issues.
5. Unwillingness to acknowledge: Taking no responsibility for mistakes or issues, not owning issues or the violation itself, placing self before the group.

6. Performance issues: Unwilling or unable to perform basic job duties, making mistakes, issues of general competence.
7. Incongruence: Misaligned with or not honoring core values, mission, practices; actions do not match words.
8. Structural issues, including changes in systems and procedures, lack of structure or too much structure, and misalignment of job duties and authority.

Trust Repair through Forgiveness

When trust has been violated, the leader must tackle the role and set the example of getting beyond the breach. Recent research suggests that the ability to forgive is a powerful way for continuance. On the receiving or victim's side of trust repair, other researchers have been investigating the role of forgiveness. Forgiveness appears to be a critical link in the trust-repair process because, through forgiveness, the victim acknowledges that some type of violation occurred, but also that the person shows regret and is committed to not repeating the violation. Forgiveness has received significant attention in recent years, from press given to the healing role played by the South African Truth and Reconciliation Commission to understanding the importance of forgiveness in the mental health rehabilitation for those who have suffered significant pain, loss, and betrayal.

Reinstatement

Reinstatement clearly relates to trust repair, in that it is the process by which trust is eventually rebuilt as acceptable explanations are provided for past actions, inappropriate behaviors are corrected, privileges to the violator are restored, situational conditions that may have contributed to the trust violation are restructured, and power is rebalanced between the parties.

In addition to verbal accounts (accounts, explanations, and apologies) and reparations, the third major area of trust repair is to change the structural arrangements that may have contributed to the trust violation, so as to serve as a deterrent and minimize the likelihood of future trust violation.

Empowering Subordinates

Competent leaders know the best way to create a solid organization is to empower subordinates. Give them a task, delegate the necessary authority, and let them do the work. Empowering the team does not mean omitting checks and making corrections when necessary. When mistakes happen, leaders ensure that followers sort out what happened and why.

Because subordinates learn best by doing, leaders should be willing to take calculated risks and accept the possibility that less experienced followers will make mistakes. If follower's leaders are to grow and develop trust, it is best to let them learn through experience. Good leaders allow space so followers can experiment within the bounds of intent-based directions and plans.

On the opposite end of the spectrum, weak leaders who have not trained their people sometimes insist, "They can't do it without me." Leaders, used to being the center of the attention, often feel indispensable, their battle cry being, "I can't take a day off. I have to be here all the time. I must watch my subordinates' every move, or who knows what will happen?" The fact is that no leader is irreplaceable. The organization will not stop functioning just because one leader, no matter how senior or central, steps aside.

Accountability is not the same as punishment.

Good Leaders Hold Followers Accountable

There is no greater act of respect for others than to hold them accountable. I am amazed at how many front-line supervisors are afraid to hold people accountable. They are afraid that moral will go down, that relationships will be strained, or that they will be perceived as hard and unreasonable.

The fact is that accountability is the ultimate demonstration of a leader's eagerness to build and uplift their followers. If done properly, it gives direction, corrects dangerously developing patterns, and helps to stretch people up and into new horizons. Accountability is a major change agent; without it nothing improves, processes become routine, and growth suffers. The greatest lessons I learned as a young leader were when I was made to account for my failures and successes.

When a leader understands accountability, what they will soon realize, is that it is the ultimate demonstration of a leader's eagerness to build and uplift their followers.

Accountability is the ultimate demonstration of a leader's eagerness to build and uplift their followers.

I learned this principle early in my career as a Company Commander in the Army, stationed in Panama.

I always insisted that my platoon leaders insure each soldier carried three days of water, food, and clothing; regardless of our mission's duration. I knew it was tempting in the tropical heat to lighten the loads, discarding items deemed unnecessary.

I made it a policy that before each mission into the jungle, I would conduct a brief inspection on one or two of the soldiers. If I discovered a light ruck-sack, I would call the Lieutenant aside and ask, "Lieutenant, help me understand why Private Miller's canteen is empty?", or whatever else was not in compliance.

I did it in private, with a calm demeanor, no barking in anger; I was holding them accountable.

As a result, our unit was a top performer. There were no injuries, everyone came home, and most importantly, the soldiers became better at what they did.

They grew professionally and in the end, recognized that holding them accountable made them better individuals.

Effective leaders understand how to hold members accountable without condemnation or excessive criticism. Leaders hold the followers accountable, not only for their actions, but for their development. Many well-meaning leaders protect their followers by withholding challenging assignments in order to avoid conflict or failure. Accountability is essential for individual development and change; it is extremely important that we set and communicate high standards. I have found that our followers tend to perform at a standard set by the leader. Where neither responsibility nor accountability is expected, growth and development stop.

The military places the concept of developing trust and confidence in its leaders, as one of the cornerstones for successful leadership. It has a field manual, FM 6-22, that suggests it's leaders continually develop their subordinates to improve their skills, keep them upward mobile, and help them become critical thinkers regarding all aspects of their mission.

They do not simply want a warm body that can carry sixty pounds on their backs and move from point A to point B in mechanical fashion. Rather, they want followers who can not only perform physically, but can also use their minds and creativity to be flexible, so that the unit as a whole may benefit. As a result of developing the whole individual, military leaders often times realize the highest levels of commitment and trust from their troops.

Setting High Standards

Setting and maintaining high standards of performance and conduct are other elements of accountability. It's okay to expect high standards from your followers. Setting high standards, both moral and technical, is a motivating experience that allows them to accomplish more than we thought was possible. This instills both individual and personal pride. Expressing and setting high expectations of performance, demonstrates a strong confidence in peoples' capabilities which inspires achievement for higher performance. As a result, there will be a desire for affiliation with the group who is number one.

> **A leader, who does not set standards for his followers, condemns them to mediocrity and self-indulgence.**

Trust is Long Term

The value of establishing trust is that it lasts a long time. It stands the pressures of every day trials and adverse events. The more authority and trust you share with front line leaders, the more efficient the organization will become. I noticed that once I restricted or took away authority, the level of performance and commitment diminished with it.

> **Effective leaders know their followers, and seek their follower's best interests above their own.**

During a training session with some managers in Texas, a manager asked me the following questions:

"What are your goals? What do you want to accomplish?"

I observed his seriousness of purpose, and answered in the same spirit, "My strongest desire is to qualify to be a friend of those whom I lead."

I had not responded to such a question in just that way before, but the answer I gave, did put into words my deepest beliefs and yearnings. Most of us are committed to our true friends, yet we are afraid to extend that commitment beyond the bounds of our private lives.

I maintain that good leaders are not afraid to make friends of their employees, a concept that raises eyebrows in the corporate world. The problem is how friendship is defined and viewed; friendship is not the same as participating in destructive indulgence and the feeding of appetites and passions.

The dictionary tells us that a friend is a person attached to another by respect and affection. A true friend makes sure that your interests are protected. Leaders can create a more inspired and committed following if they understand the individual worth of each follower, and also understand the needs and individuality of the followers. Therefore, great leaders are not afraid to make friendships with their followers and to use friendship qualities to protect and develop them.

> **"I destroy my enemy when I make him my friend".**
> *Abraham Lincoln*

True friendship carries a great deal of responsibility and is not a casual exercise. True friendship embraces quality interactions and a desire to seek each other's best interests. Viewing their relationships as true and dedicated friends, help to create an environment for new opportunities, support, and a working atmosphere in which individual differences are recognized. The results are usually visible, our daily greetings become meaningful, the other person's success becomes important to us, and their personal and professional problems become a little more important.

There will be a desire to coach and communicate frankly with their followers and mentor them to success. They want them to be successful and achieve greater success; **even if it puts them ahead of and above them.**

Leaders who consider the personal needs and beliefs of their members, have a much better chance of showing individual respect and worth. That in turn, directly creates commitment and a show of respect from the members.

Recognition is one of the most powerful tools available to a leader. Every man and/or woman in the armed forces, industry, or business world, is unique and has an internal mechanism that craves attention and recognition. In nearly every job I have worked at, very few of my immediate supervisors knew much about me or my skills; other than what was within the scope of my job. Most employees are walking gold mines with talents and abilities that go untapped because leaders fail to get close to them.

Trust Is a Powerful Experience

When I was in the ninth grade, the principal of the school called my name over the intercom. "Ed Shelton," he said, "could you please come to the office?"

Everyone looked at me as I nervously made my way out of the classroom, down the hall and into the principal's office. My mind was racing, as I tried to figure out what I might have done wrong. I couldn't think of anything, but I was sure that having the principal call you to his office was usually not a good sign. The principal was not only the principal, but also the football coach.

Mr. Freedman explained that he was going to hand out new play books to the team that afternoon. "I need the books to hand out," he explained, "and I've left them in my apartment. Could you please go and get them for me?" I sighed, a sigh of relief. He then handed me the key to his apartment, and said, "This will let you in the front door. I left the books in my living room. When you leave, be sure to lock the door behind you."

Vicenza High School was an American school in Italy and had a dormitory next door where Mr. Freedman had a small apartment. I walked the short distance to his apartment; I held the key in my hand. It represented a great trust the principle had placed in me. He had chosen me as someone he could depend upon. That trust he placed in me felt good.

Building trust helps to build strong bonds between people, but we must earn that trust. Leaders must work to build it first, not the other way around.

My brother Ken was four years older than I was. He was my idol; I wanted to be just like him. I would follow him and his friends around and, although I am sure he sometimes thought of me as a little pest, he was good to me and allowed me to tag along.

When Ken was in high school, he had saved enough money to buy himself a paper route. I remember well the day he came home and announced his new business venture. It was his pride and joy, and he spent many months saving the money to buy this route. One day as we were coming home, he stopped at the bus stop and asked me if I would like to help with the route. Of course I would! I couldn't believe that he would trust me to pick up and deliver the papers— I knew how much it meant to him.

I arose, hours before school, and went down to the corner where I waited for the delivery of the papers. Other boys were there too waiting for the drop. I was the youngest, least experienced one there, but I recall how proud I was that my brother had trusted me.

I worked hard to remain trusted, I made mistakes, but my brother never lost his trust in me. I was always grateful that he understood that there would be human errors and that it hadn't destroyed his trust in me.

Leaders must understand that trusting others means along with the opportunities come challenges. It is not only important to place trust in others, but it is important to know whom you can trust. You will learn many things and will need to make choices that will sometimes be difficult. You need to place your trust in those who will to do what is right. The biggest mistake you can ever make as a leader is to never trust anyone.

In conclusion, the importance of these issues of effective trust repair and trust enhancement cannot be overstated. If trust really is the vital lubricant that facilitates organizational transactions and promotes organizational development, then the absence of such trust is disruptive and costly. To this point, the scorecard remains discouraging. In a recent appraisal of the state of trust within contemporary U.S. organizations, Americans have grown almost accustomed to lack of trustworthiness from business and government. Americans have habituated so much to the routine abuse of their trust, that it has become almost a default assumption. A survey conducted by the Center for Public Leadership reported that when asked to indicate the extent to which they trusted what leaders of organizations had to say, more than 50% indicated "not much" or "not at all" when it comes to business leaders, and 70% indicated "not much" or "not at all" when it comes to media leaders. In fact, in a sample of 20 major nations, respondents in every case reported significantly less trust in business today than even a year ago. Within the United States, moreover, respondents indicated not only sharply declining trust in general, but also sharply diminishing expectations that business will "do what is right" in addressing the trust deficit. Trust in U.S. business experienced a staggering 20-point drop from 58% to 38%.

Chapter 7

Motivation

Improving Individual Performance

How to motivate people is not a mystery nor is it limited to people who have the knack for it. It is understandable, observable and can be a tool to any leader who wishes to take the time to study it.

Motivating people is the most common problem in any society. Unlike machinery that malfunctions and the solution is replacing the broken or worn part, people are much more complicated and fixing the problem requires skill and deep understanding of how people are motivated.

Motivation is not a secret

Motivating people is no secret, we know the cause and effect for motivation and yet 80% of bosses can't seem to do it. Behavioral psychologists have long known that motivation is more than rewarding or punishing actions, that's easy but highly ineffective. The foundation for effective motivations can be found in several early studies from:

Herzberg
Hawthorne
Maslow
McGregor

Herzberg "Motivation-Hygiene Theory"

Herzberg attended City College of New York, but left part way through his studies to enlist in the army. As a patrol sergeant, he was a firsthand witness of the Dachau concentration camp. He believed that this experience, as well as the talks he had with other Germans living in the area was what triggered his interest in motivation. Herzberg graduated from City College in 1946 and moved to the University of Pittsburgh to undertake post-graduate workplace while teaching as a professor of psychology at Case Western Reserve University in Cleveland and later moved to the University of Utah where he held the position of professor of management in the college of business

Mr. Herzberg was honored in 1994 with a Distinguished Service Award at the U. from what is now the David Eccles School of Business. As a patrol sergeant during World War II, he was among the first liberators to enter the Dachau concentration camp. His decorations included the Bronze Star and the Combat Infantryman's Badge.

He proposed several key findings as a result of this identification. People are made dissatisfied by a bad environment, but they are seldom made satisfied by a good environment. The prevention of dissatisfaction is just as important as encouragement of motivator satisfaction. Hygiene factors operate independently of motivation factors. An individual can be highly motivated in his work and be dissatisfied with his work environment. All hygiene factors are equally important, although their frequency of occurrence differs considerably. Hygiene improvements have short-term effects. Any improvements result in a short-term removal of, or prevention of, dissatisfaction. Hygiene needs are cyclical in nature and come back to a starting point. This leads to the "What have you done for me lately?" syndrome.

Herzberg Motivation Model

People are made dissatisfied by a bad environment, but they are seldom made satisfied by a good environment.

The prevention of dissatisfaction is just as important as encouragement of motivator satisfaction.

Hygiene factors operate independently of motivation factors. An individual can be highly motivated in his work and be dissatisfied with his work environment.

All hygiene factors are equally important, although their frequency of occurrence differs considerably.

Hygiene improvements have short-term effects. Any improvements result in a short-term removal of, or prevention of, dissatisfaction.

Hygiene needs are cyclical in nature and come back to a starting point. This leads to the "What have you done for me lately?" syndrome.

Hygiene needs have an escalating zero point and no final answer.

Leaders Motivate

Motivation comes from within, but is affected by others' actions and words. A leader's role in motivation is to understand the needs and desires of others, to align and elevate individual drives into team goals, and to influence others and accomplish those larger aims. Some followers have high levels of internal motivation to get a job done, while others need more reassurance and feedback. Motivation spurs initiative when something needs to be accomplished.

When followers succeed, praise them. When they fall short, give them credit for what they have done right, but advise them on how to do better. When motivating with words, leaders should use more than just empty phrases; they should personalize the message.

Indirect approaches can be as successful as what is said. Setting a personal example can sustain the drive in others. This becomes apparent when leaders share the hardships. When a problem arises within the organization, all key leaders should be involved to share in the hard work to get the problem fixed. This includes leadership presence at night, weekends, and in all locations and conditions where the employees are toiling.

The ability to motivate is a key element of leadership. Defining and understanding motivation seems to be unclear for many managers who usually know that it is important to achieve improved performance. Leaders, who understand motivation, tend to first understand and possess four fundamental leadership qualities that include the following:

Personal Qualities for Leadership

Intelligence

Love of Learning

Power of Introspection

Respect for People

Intelligence

Leader's intelligence draws on the mental tendencies and resources that shape conceptual abilities, which are applied to duties and responsibilities. Conceptual abilities enable sound judgment before implementing concepts and plans. They help one think creatively and reason analytically, critically, ethically, and with cultural sensitivity to consider unintended as well as intended consequences. Like a chess player trying to anticipate an opponent's moves three or four turns in advance (action-reaction counteraction), leaders must think through what they expect to occur because of a decision. Some decisions may set off a chain of events. Therefore, leaders must attempt to anticipate the second—and third-order effects of their actions. However, intelligence alone must be merged and balanced with five fundamental cognitive skills.

Necessary Cognitive Skills

Mental Agility

Sound Judgment

Innovation

Interpersonal tact

Domain knowledge

Mental Agility

Mental agility is a flexibility of mind, a tendency to anticipate or adapt to uncertain or changing situations. Agility assists thinking through second—and third-order effects when current decisions or actions are not producing the desired effects. It helps break from habitual thought patterns, to improvise when faced with conceptual impasses, and quickly apply multiple perspectives to consider new approaches or solutions.

Mental agility is important in leadership because agile leaders stay ahead of changing environments and incomplete planning to preempt problems. In the operational sense, agility also shows in the ability to create ad hoc and creative teams that adapt to changing situations. They can alter their behavior to ease transitioning and change.

The basis for mental agility is the ability to reason critically while keeping an open mind to multiple possibilities until reaching the most sensible solution. Critical thinking is a thought process that aims to find truth in situations where direct observation is insufficient, impossible, or impractical. It allows thinking through and solving problems and is central to decision making. Critical thinking is the key to understanding changing situations, finding causes, arriving at justifiable conclusions, making good judgments, and learning from experience.

Critical thinking implies examining a problem in depth, from multiple points of view, and not settling for the first answer that comes to mind. Leaders need this ability because many of the choices they face require more than one solution. The first and most important step in finding an appropriate solution is to isolate the main problem. Sometimes determining the real problem presents a huge hurdle; at other times, one has to sort through distracting multiple problems to get to the real issue.

A leader's mental agility in quickly isolating a problem and identifying solutions allows the use of initiative to adjust to change during operations. Agility and initiative do not appear magically. The leader must instill them within all followers by creating a climate that encourages team participation.

Identifying and dealing appropriately with honest mistakes makes followers more likely to develop their own initiative.

Sound Judgment

Judgment goes hand in hand with agility. Judgment requires having a capacity to assess situations or circumstances shrewdly and to draw feasible conclusions. Good judgment enables the leader to form sound opinions and to make sensible decisions and reliable guesses. Good judgment on a consistent basis is important for successful leaders and much of it comes from experience. Leaders acquire experience through trial and error and by watching the experiences of others. Learning from others can occur through mentoring and coaching by the boss, peers, and even other followers or peers. Another method of expanding experience is self-development by reading biographies and autobiographies of notable businessmen and women to learn from their successes and failures. The histories of successful people offer ageless insights, wisdom, and methods that might be adaptable to the current environment or situation.

Often, leaders must juggle facts, questionable data, and gut-level feelings to arrive at a quality decision. Good judgment helps to make the best decision for the situation at hand. It is a key attribute of the art of transformation of knowledge into understanding and quality execution.

Good judgment contributes to an ability to determine possible courses of action and decide what action to take. Before choosing the course of action, consider the consequences and think methodically. Some sources that aid judgment are senior leaders' intents, the desired outcome, rules, laws, regulations, experience, and values. Good judgment includes the ability to size up followers and peers for strengths, weaknesses, and to create appropriate solutions and action. Like agility, it is a critical part of problem solving and decision making.

Innovation

Innovation describes the leader's ability to introduce something new for the first time when needed or an opportunity exists. Being innovative includes creativity in the production of ideas that are original and worthwhile.

Sometimes a new problem presents itself or an old problem requires a new solution. Leaders should seize such opportunities to think creatively and to innovate. The key concept for creative thinking is developing new ideas and ways to challenge followers with new approaches and ideas. It also involves devising new ways for workers to accomplish task and job requirements. Creative thinking includes using adaptive approaches (drawing from previous similar circumstances) or innovative approaches (coming up with a completely new idea).

Leader Intelligence

Innovative leaders prevent complacency by finding new ways to challenge followers with forward-looking approaches and ideas. To be innovators, leaders learn to rely on intuition, experience, knowledge, and input from followers. Innovative leaders reinforce team building by making everybody responsible for and stakeholders in, the innovation process.

Interpersonal Tact

Effectively interacting with others depends on knowing what others perceive. It also relies on accepting the character, reactions, and motives of oneself and others. Interpersonal tact combines these skills, along with recognizing diversity and displaying self-control, balance, and stability in all situations.

Recognition Diversity

The workforce is made up of people who originate from vastly different backgrounds and are shaped by schooling, race, gender, religion, as well as a host of other influences. Personal perspectives can even vary within societal groups. People should avoid snap conclusions based on stereotypes. It is better to understand individuals by acknowledging their differences, qualifications, contributions, and potential.

Joining the Organization, we all agree to accept the Organizational culture. This initial bond holds them together. Leaders further strengthen the team effort by creating an environment where followers know they are valued for their talents, contributions, and differences. A leader's job is not to make everyone the same; it is to take advantage of the different capabilities and talents brought to the team. The biggest challenge is to put each member in the right place to build the best possible team.

Leaders must keep an open mind about cultural diversity. It is important, because it is unknown how the talents of certain individuals or groups will contribute to mission accomplishment. During World War II, U.S. Marines from the Navajo nation formed a group of radio communications specialists called the Navajo Code Talkers. The code talkers used their native language—a unique talent—to handle command radio traffic. Using the Navajo code significantly contributed to successful ground operations because the best Japanese code breakers could not decipher their messages.

Self-Control

Effective front line leaders control their emotions. Instead of hysterics or showing no emotion at all, leaders should display the right amount of sensitivity and passion to tap into subordinates' emotions. Maintaining self-control inspires calm confidence in the team. Self-control encourages feedback from subordinates that can expand understanding of what is really happening. Self-control in combat is especially important for leaders. Leaders who lose their self-control cannot expect those who follow them to maintain theirs.

A leader's emotional state is often transferred to subordinates. A Plant Manager at Mountain City Meat Company demonstrates how short tempers, fatigue, and stress can have a devastating effect.

Leaders do not have the luxury of being able to lose their temper, be unprofessional, or berate subordinate leaders and followers. Every action is noticed and although some followers dismissed the incident, some carried the memory throughout their career.

> It is impossible for any leader who loses his temper and flies into a tantrum to obtain commitment from his followers.

Importance of Self Control

During a startup operation for a new processing line at a hamburger processing facility, Pat Boyer the owner had been under a lot of stress and had gotten little sleep.

Pat had earned a reputation for a short temper, but nothing prepared the plant personnel for what happened next.

Pat had snapped, causing a commotion on one of the lines: "You need to get your people under control; that idiot Smith (the line supervisor) is nowhere around and this line is not ready to go, we have 10 minutes, it'll be a disaster. Who does he think he is?"

A fellow line supervisor tried to calm the situation down by offering to give Pat the reassurance that he could make sure that the line would be organized and start on time.

"No! I want MY SUPERVISOR NOW! When that idiot gets back I want him standing right here," kicking his heel into the concrete floor "No break, no excuses, he better be waiting for me when I get back."

The "idiot" had been with his employees giving them preoperational instructions and briefing them for the day's quotas and finding out what problems they were facing on the line. He had also stopped by the tool room to discuss some underperforming machinery that needed to be fixed. He was doing his job.

Pat Boyer was obviously overstressed by the situation, his job, and the demanding pace of the operations, just like everyone else on the plant staff.

His failure to control his anger and maintain his professional bearing cost him the respect and loyalty of many of his fellow managers and employees on the line. It also planted a seed of doubt about how he would perform under similar stressful situations.

Pat Boyer's blunder served employees differently that day. Some saw the effects of stress and its impacts and some saw something they never wanted to become.

Anyone can get angry—that is easy . . . but to get angry with the right person, to the right extent, at the right time, for the right reason, and in the right way is no longer something easy that anyone can do.

Aristotle

Emotional Factors

A leader's self-control, balance, and stability greatly influence his ability to interact with others. People are human beings with hopes, fears, concerns, and dreams. Understanding that motivation and endurance are sparked by emotional energy is a powerful leadership tool. Giving constructive feedback will help mobilize the team's emotional energies to accomplish difficult missions during tough times.

Self-control, balance, and stability also assist making the right ethical choices. An ethical leader successfully applies ethical principles to decision making and retains self-control. Leaders cannot be at the mercy of emotion. It is critical for leaders to remain calm under pressure and expend energy on things they can positively influence and not worry about things they cannot affect.

Emotionally mature and competent leaders are also aware of their own strengths and weaknesses. They spend their energy on self-improvement, while immature leaders usually waste their energy denying that there is anything wrong or analyzing the shortcomings of others. Mature, less defensive leaders benefit from feedback in ways that immature people cannot.

Balance

Emotionally balanced leaders are able to display the right emotion for a given situation and can read others' emotional state. They draw on their experience and provide their subordinates the proper perspective on unfolding events. They have a range of attitudes, from relaxed to intense, with which to approach diverse situations. They know how to choose the one appropriate for the circumstances. Balanced leaders know how to convey that things are urgent without throwing the entire organization into chaos. They are able to encourage their people to continue the assignments, even in the toughest of moments.

Effective leaders are steady, levelheaded when under pressure and fatigued, and calm in the face of management pressure. These characteristics stabilize their subordinates who are always looking to their leader's example:

1. **Model the emotions for subordinates to display.**

2. **Do not give in to the temptation to do what personally feels good.**

3. **If under great stress, it might feel better to vent—but will that help the organization?**

4. **If subordinates are to be calm and rational under pressure, leaders must display the same stability.**

Keeping Emotions Balanced

I came to understand this principle while serving as a Second Lieutenant stationed on the DMZ in Korea.

We had received a mission order to set up a company size ambush. A large number of North Korean sappers were moving toward the capital of Seoul via the DMZ to conduct assassination missions.

I was to move my platoon forward and set up; another platoon would follow and establish contact on my right flank. The third platoon would stay behind and provide security and act as the reserve force.

Within hours my platoon was in place but the platoon behind me was being delayed by heavy rains and several solders that had become disoriented.

As I monitored the radio traffic, I could hear our Company Commander, Captain Parsons yelling "Where the f—are you, get you're a—in place now!

My colleagues LT Bates replied with equal cursing and intensity. The excitement and tension of the mission had been escalated by the Captains lack of control, he had created the environment.

I personally started to question the wisdom and decision making of Captain Parsons and started to rely more on my own instincts and less on the wisdom and skills of my Captain.

That day made me realize how important the leader's ability to control his emotions are and how its impact can be devastating or beneficial to the organization.

Common Sense Knowledge

Common sense knowledge requires possessing facts, beliefs, and logical assumptions in many areas. Skills or technical knowledge is an understanding of technical information, tools and procedures related to production systems and methods. Technical knowledge consists of the specialized information associated with a particular function or system. Joint knowledge is an understanding of joint organizations, their procedures, and their roles in national defense. Cultural and geopolitical knowledge is awareness of cultural, geographic, and political differences and sensitivities.

Technical Knowledge

Technical knowledge relates to equipment, and systems—everything from line equipment to the computer that tracks product or personnel actions. Since front line leaders are closer to their equipment or machinery than organizational and strategic leaders, they have a greater need to know how it works and how to use it. Front line leaders are usually the experts called upon to solve problems with equipment. They figure out how to make it work better, how to apply it, how to fix it, and even how to modify it. If they do not know the specifics, they will know who knows how to solve issues with it. Followers expect their front line leaders to know the equipment and be experts in all the applicable technical skills.

Leader Intelligence

Leaders know how to operate their organizations' equipment and ensure their people do as well. They often set an example with a hands-on approach. When new equipment arrives, direct leaders learn how to use it and train their followers to do the same. Once individuals are trained, teams, and in turn, whole units train together. Leaders know understanding equipment strengths and weaknesses are critical. Adapting to these factors is necessary to achieve business.

Intelligence is not just a matter of what IQ you are born with; intelligence can be increased through determined application and study. I have heard front-line managers say that they are not smart enough to lead or figure something out. They may come from home environments that reinforce this idea, and may tend to believe that no matter what happens, they have no control over how smart they are. The fact is, that intelligence is accumulated knowledge and can be added upon through reading, experiences, and observation. There is absolutely no need for anyone to go through their career resolved to not learn or grow. Leading others requires knowledge and learning.

Abraham Lincoln was a product of the backwoods of early America. He lost his mother at an early age and grew up with a father who belittled him and called him lazy. Through perseverance, he determined to self-educate himself and become a great lawyer and president.

Without opportunity for formal schooling, Abraham Lincoln was interested in almost every subject. He went from a backwoods nobody, to become a lawyer, state senator, and eventually President of the United States; all achieved without a formal education. He was a leader who achieved great things for the people and the country.

Eagerness to Learning

There is a second quality; a quality that you and I must have if we want to become effective leaders. It is a zeal for learning our trade or profession.

Benjamin Franklin, Abraham Lincoln, and all great public and business leaders I have met, are of like nature. Throughout their lives, a zeal for learning was one of their greatest qualities. Their zeal became continuous with these leaders, never wavering.

Power of Introspection

Most great leaders have another quality that is important to all of us. It is the power of introspection—the power to look within ourselves and see what kind of person we are.

Every morning, each one of us looks into a mirror to examine our physical appearance—hair styling, makeup, general health. Have you ever thought how fine it would be to look within yourself—to meet yourself on the street and ask yourself what kind of a person you are, to interrogate yourself? Do you know your own faults, your own strengths?

Here is an interesting quality of most leaders who trust and are trusted. They know their own weaknesses and strengths, and they work to develop their weaknesses into strengths.

Most of us hide our weaknesses. In the business world, I have witnessed many, good managers and workers destined for failure, due to fully following the directions and instructions, given them by their boss. It is at these moments, lesser leaders do not acknowledge their errors, and try to hide their weaknesses or failures. Effective leaders accept the reprimands, acknowledge and correct the errors, building greater trust in the process.

As leaders, it is important and okay to recognize that we have many weaknesses, but we must set about to overcome them.

Respect for People

Let me refer to another characteristic of an effective leader which has been a key theme in this book: *respect for people.*

No leader can be great in this world without a deep respect for those who work for them. The challenge for the leader in any organization is to engage in the kinds of actions that will let those who work with or under him, know that he has a vital, personal concern about them as individuals.

No organization can exist for long unless work is completed, and goals are accomplished. The leader cannot ignore work-centered activities, and he should see that activities are planned, programs are set up, materials are in order, and assignments are made and followed through. But all of this must be done in the general atmosphere of an overriding concern for those who must do the work and carry out the assignments. When people feel like their superiors think the work is more important than the people who do it, motivation to work is hindered.

This is the critical balance—good planning, organization, and high performance standards for work, in an atmosphere where each individual involved feels confident that he, personally, is understood, appreciated, and highly involved.

What can be done by leaders to create an atmosphere of personal concern and individual acceptance?

Four Principles on Becoming a Leader of Genuine Concern

Take time

Too often the interaction at work is hurried, poorly timed, and conducted with the feeling, "We're both busy, so let's hurry and get this over with." Find little bits of time regularly, for quick expressions of appreciation, an interview, or an oral evaluation. These should be scheduled with time enough to express real appreciation, to find out any personal concerns, and to talk about, not only the job, but also the person.

Ask personal questions

For many reasons, leaders shy away from talking personally with others. It seems safer to talk business. But one can move into the area of personal concern by saying something like the following: "I honestly would like to know how you feel about your work, and if it conflicts with your family. If you have any qualms or reservations, I would like to know; and if you have any suggestions for improving things, they would be most welcome," or "How are things going for you now? Do you having any problems, questions, or difficulties with which I can help?"

It may be possible to open up a discussion of something you, the leader, have noticed is bothering the other person.

Listen with understanding

If a person begins to talk about feelings of concern about matters that affect him, the leader must listen, and listen, and listen; then try to understand. It will not be helpful if the leader invites sharing and then interrupts with such comments as, "That's not how it really is,"; "You didn't really get a clear picture of what we are trying to do,"; "Let me tell you what I would do if I was you," or "That's not the way we do things here."

They can listen with understanding or empathy. This means honestly trying to see the problem or the situation from the other person's position, and to try to understand how and why he sees and responds to things the way he does. This way, help can be given from where *he* is rather than from where the *leader* is.

Be willing to do something

One of the most common reactions of the leader after a person has shared a real concern is to ask, "How can I help?"

This question often puts the person being interviewed in a real dilemma. He may not have been asking for help, and he may not know what would be the appropriate thing to say.

Feeling awkward and embarrassed he may say, "Oh, I don't need any help," or "I don't know what you could do."

Instead of asking what he can do, the leader can actually do something: he can take action. He can express understanding, concern, and empathy. He can respond with an expression of support or gratitude, a touch or a pat on the back. He can suggest action, such as: "I know that this project is difficult; let me go to the production line this week see it for myself." "That's a tough problem. Let me talk to the president and get his reaction."

If one has real concern, he can usually do something that reflects through his actions that his concern is real, and not just a ploy used because he has read an article on personal concern and feels he ought to try it.

Do your workers behave the way you expect them to behave? Is their behavior based upon your attitude toward them? Is honest praise a good motivational and directional force?

Self-Fulfilling Prophecy

Research suggests that the answer is yes. Your attitude as a leader creates the environment in which your workers exist. A leader becomes an environmental creator. For example, quite unconsciously, leaders interact with their workers so that they may receive the response they expect to receive. If you continually tell a child he is lazy and no good, you will have a lazy no good child. If you tell a worker that things are not working out, things will not work out. Self-fulfilling prophecy applied in negative terms can kill the workforce.

Self-fulfilling Prophecy Study

Several years ago, I was part of a study that examined leadership aptitude of over one hundred immigrant workers, and over one hundred non-immigrant workers at a production plant.

At random, five percent of the workers from each department were selected as an experimental group. Their managers were told that these particular workers had scored high on the leadership test and would show remarkable gains in leadership development during the next few months.

Actually, the only difference between these workers and the others in the plant was in the minds of the production managers.

By the end of six months, the workers designated as "talented", had received higher performance reviews than did the other workers in the other group.

The department managers and supervisors were asked to describe the work behavior of their "talented" workers. They were seen as harder working, more detailed, and responsive.

> **Studies of this nature demonstrate the widespread tendency of people to behave the way others expect them to behave; a pattern known as the self-fulfilling prophecy.**
>
> **If we really believe that people will behave in a certain way, then our attitude is based on that expectation. In turn, our attitude produces the expected behavior.**

As a leader I decided early in my career that I would not use casual phrases that undermine, degrade others or suggest failure to others. If it was not uplifting and positive, I would leave the issue alone.

Literature and research, suggest that positive feedback, honest praise, and recognition for work well done, reinforce self-motivation and make people feel good. Negative reactions and the assignments of tasks beyond one's abilities, can break down both a person's self-motivation and his self-esteem.

This cycle develops into a vicious circle, where a manager or supervisor perceiving a worker is a poor performer, lazy or does not care, treats the worker accordingly; and the worker will respond accordingly. This response reinforces the manager's attitude and a completely negative relationship ensues.

If leaders seek and exploit the workers better qualities, and act as though the worker is a valuable part of the team offering honest praise for work well done, then the worker will most likely react favorably and a positive relationship exists.

The VP of Human Resources was coming to visit for the first time. I was somewhat anxious about this first visit, since I didn't know him very well personally. I was relatively young and inexperienced, and didn't want anything to undermine the confidence placed in me. Frankly, I was somewhat guarded and apprehensive.

However, from our first meeting, the president's attitude was, "What are you trying to accomplish and how can I help you?"

His sincerity totally disarmed me. I felt he was there to help me, not to judge me. I therefore freely shared our problems and goals and asked for his help, and I had available the invaluable resources of a very experienced, wise, and effective leader.

During his visit, I invited him to join me and my staff of 12 for a meeting to discuss some important union issues. I remember that during the meeting, some of the staff began voicing concerns and looked to our guest for sympathy.

He answered, in substance, "These, of course, are for Ed's attention. I'm here to sustain and help him. He will have to deal with these concerns that you have expressed."

Responsibility for improving leadership skills is the responsibility of the manager or leader themselves and those appointed over them. However, it is the leader who is the only one, in the last analysis, who can break the self-fulfilling cycle.

Supporting vs. Meddling

There is nothing more debilitating than for someone who manages or leads others to meddle. Meddling is the act of controlling and directing in a way that disrupts the natural or designed flow of administration and governance. For those who are affected by meddling bosses, it is demotivating and discouraging.

What would have happened if he had been openly sympathetic with some of their views? Where would they have looked for leadership? Not to him, for he was returning to Virginia, and had many HR divisions to supervise. He couldn't possibly get involved on a regular basis in details of local affairs. Instead, I felt sustained. How responsible I felt! How committed! How motivated to make things work! How open I was to his advice and ideas and help! If I had doubts or questions about the sincere concerns raised, I would privately ask him. His basic answer was, "You might consider what they're doing in this or that issue." This left me with the decision and the responsibility.

Those who have worked with hovering supervisors know how it undermines one's sense of responsibility and initiative. You simply can't delegate responsibility for results and supervise methods very closely. If you do, you take back the responsibility.

It is far better to teach correct management principles, and let those under you make decisions themselves in light of those principles. Then you have built all your judgments into those principles and you become their helper, their leader. Even if they falter or fail altogether, you always return to discuss the original assignment or agreement, and either revise it or renew it together.

Critical to ensuring that people are allowed to act and make decisions, is the leaders' willingness to self-examine oneself. Self-examination is most difficult. Surveys have shown that most people take credit for success to themselves, but blame their failures on external forces or other people. It would be well, when confronted with a problem, to be able to ask—is the problem me?

Leadership requires the application of self-examination, and to have the courage, fortitude, and wisdom to apply self-examination. Or will you, as many do, be inclined to try and decide which of your associates will fail.

People must be allowed to make mistakes and learn from those experiences as well as from others mistakes. Tolerance for mistakes takes patience and wisdom not raw emotional reasoning. The greatest lessons in life have come from failure and we must allow reasonable failure for people to become better.

Committed leaders will not permit those under them to engage in destructive criticism, retaliation, or undue disgust. We should commit ourselves to marching, shoulder to shoulder, with our workers—without destroying, condemning, or belittling.

> **An employee at a gas plant in Saudi Arabia, where I served on the management team, fell off of an oil platform he was working on.**
>
> **To my question, "Why did you fall of the platform?" he replied, "I fell out because I wasn't in far enough!" Employees, who fall "out" of the workforce, were never "in" far enough.**
>
> **The leaders failed to insure that the employee's best interests were met, and they never felt they were accepted as part of the team. They have not been made a part of the social dynamics or the team.**

In a simple statement, the difference between those leaders who are committed and those who are not, is the difference between the words *want* and *will*.

For example, "I want to be an effective leader, but the employees are too lazy or hard to work with," or "I will be effective and make sure I create the proper environment and provide the proper tools for them to be successful." "I would like to be a good leader, but look what I have to work with" or "I will be an effective and good leader."

Chapter 8

Leading by Fear

King's Son

When King Solomon died his young son ascended to the throne. The new king called a counsel together to discuss the future of his reign.

The old and experienced men spoke to him, saying, if you will be a servant unto the people and serve them, and answer them, and speak kind words to them, then they will follow you forever.

But he forsook the counsel of the old men, which they had given him, and consulted with the young men he had grown up with, and who he sought counsel from them.

He asked them, what counsel can you give me regarding the people, who have spoken to me, saying, make the yoke which thy father did put upon us lighter?

And the young men spoke unto him, saying, and now whereas your father did lade the subjects with a heavy yoke—add to their yoke: your father hath chastised them with whips, but you will chastise them with scorpions. (Clearly suggesting harsher treatment fear and tyranny.)

> **The king gathered his entire subjects around and talked to the people roughly, and ignored the old men's counsel that they gave him and acted on the council of the younger men.**
>
> **Eventually this king lost more than half of his kingdom through rebellion and fighting, never to see the kingdom in its fullness again for all time.**

One of the most oft-observed failures of leadership comes when we place too much emphasis on being recognized as a leader. Thinking that we are more important or powerful than others can be perilous to us and to those we lead. It is vital that we not become trapped by the enticement of recognition or thinking that we are above the rest, using fear to reinforce this attitude is disastrous.

Do not let praise and self-importance go to your head. Adulation is poison. If you can do that, you'll get along all right and will go forward with a love for the people and a great respect for them and in turn you will be a leader of great value.

There is an account of the Kings Son who lost his vision of his father's pattern of leadership while trying to protect his own leadership position and who rejected the counsel of the old men that stood before him to lighten the burden of the people. Instead, he imposed additional hardships on them thinking that he could establish order and retain his hold over the people by means of fear.

The story continues and ends with the young son's focus on his own might led to continuous contention with the leaders of other tribes. The northern tribes felt threatened by his actions and appointed an opposing King who went to war ending in not only a split kingdom but weakened by civil war was conquered by the Babylonians never to arise again as a free nation.

A leader who depends on fear, reward systems, regulations, policy, position and the power of disciplinary action to motivate and carry out assignments, simply does not understand what motivation is. Known in the academic circles as transactional or implicit contracting leadership, this is the most commonly applied leadership style and the least effective. It is what separates effective leaders from average and ineffective leaders. It creates a relationship based on explicit contracts or a *quid pro qua* (. . . I will give you this in exchange for that) relationship. It is conditional, and tends to defocus on the individual and more on the system.

Many leaders fail because of power-dominance; having a real or perceived need to dominate those under them. Triggered by attitudes or learned behavior, domination is a self-centered attribute that drives leaders to seek their own interests over their follower's. The problem is that most followers easily and quickly recognize domination as being self-centered, and resist either passively or openly.

The HMS Bounty

Captain Bligh was the Captain of the HMS Bounty. Shortly after departing England, the Captain was confronted by the ships logistical officer, who reports that there is some cheese missing. Capt. Bligh ordered the rations to be cut until the shortage is made up.

As Captain Bligh and Mr. Christian were going down below, they overhear a sailor accusing Capt. Bligh of stealing the cheese. Confronting the sailor, he asks Mr. Christianson what he recommends, to which Mr. Christianson suggests two weeks without grog. Capt. Bligh orders the man to be punished with twenty-four lashes in front of the crew. On deck, the punishment is about to begin, when the designated, whipping sailor leans over and whispers to the accused, "Remember it's not me", to which the sailor replies, "It's okay, I can take it".

The lashing begins and by the twelfth lash, all are becoming squeamish and visibly disturbed with the brutality of the punishment. The sailor is taken down and the crew dismissed.

That evening at Officer Mess, Captain Bligh sees that the officers appetites are wanting and asks Mr. Christianson what the problem is and to speak freely. Mr., Christian tells Bligh that he felt the punishment was too severe. Capt. Bligh then gives a lecture to the officers: "You will all be Captains in charge of your own ship one day. Let me describe the typical seaman. He is half-witted, a wife-beater, a habitual drunkard, and he spends his whole life evading and defying authority. What makes this man go aloft? I tell you, its fear. Now, I'm not a man for cruelty or barbarism, but cruelty with purpose is not cruelty, its efficiency. A man will never disobey you when once he's seen his mate's backbone laid bare, he'll remember those white ribs staring at him; he'll see the flesh jump, hear the whistle of the whip for the rest of his life".

Mr. Christian ponders this lecture for several minutes then proclaims, "Perhaps you are right. (There is a long pause as Captain Bligh picks up a sliver of cheese). I would be careful with that cheese if I were you sir, it has a peculiar smell. I believe it's a bit tainted. But of course, it's a matter if individual taste."

In a diplomatic way, Mr. Christiansen has pointed out that he does not agree with Bligh's style of leadership. This particular episode describes many leaders who believe in "motivation by fear".

Stalin Leading by Fear

It has been speculated that under Stalin's leadership, more people were put to death for political and cultural reasons than during Hitler's invasion. Stalin's methods were fear-based. He believed that fear was necessary in order to accomplish his vision of Russia's future. Under his orders during WW II, he ordered the organization of the NKVD, a Para-military group that searched the war zones and adjacent areas for deserters or malingerers, and summarily execute them.

His reign of terror began in 1936 and ended at his death in 1939. Stalin's leadership led to over two million, soviet citizens being placed in concentration camp Gulag's, where they would die of starvation, forced labor, and exposure from the harsh Siberian winters.

Nikita Khrushchev's "Secret Speech"

In 1956, Nikita Khrushchev delivered a blistering speech about the tyranny of Joseph Stalin. The speech broke Stalin's spell, by telling the truth about his crimes and began the process that abolished the Soviet Union thirty years later.

In Nikita Khrushchev's 1956 speech, he addressed the soviet political elites with an off-the record speech that renounced Stalin and his dogma. It was a denunciation of Stalin and his actions against the Soviet people.

The speech shocked many of the communist hard liners in attendance. Then, somewhere in the crowd, came a pointed question from one of the younger communist members. "If you knew what was going on, why didn't you do something?"

Nikita glared out at the audience and, slamming his closed fist onto the podium he demanded, "Who said that?" Silence . . . not a man spoke. He demanded again, slamming his fist on the podium harder, "Tell me, who said that."

Again, not a stir, no one dared stand up or say a word. Khrushchev yelled into the microphone, pointing his finger at the assembly, "I want to know, who said that, now!" The silence was penetrating.

After several minutes, he leaned forward and in a firm, audible whisper he said, "That's why we did nothing."

These strong willed Soviet leaders were brought to their knees because of fear.

The problem with leading by fear is that it is temporary and cannot be sustained; it requires perpetuating the fear factor, which in turn causes resentment and loss of trust and respect from the followers. It is similar to a brutish father who uses capital punishment on his children; they will immediately obey today, but tomorrow they will despise and resent his brutality.

To help better understand this concept of leading by fear and the negative aspects that it brings to people and relationships, I have developed the following comparison for you to review. You will see that those qualities under the Tyrannical Leader are undesirable and cannot be uplifting or positive. So why do leaders in today's workplace feel fear is appropriate?

Reviewing historical leaders such as Hitler, Custer, Stalin and some bosses you may have worked for, the question is, why did they use fear? The answer may be that they saw fear as leadership strength, and in every case, nothing they achieved was helpful to the organization or its leadership. Not one of them was trusted or respected by their followers. They did okay in getting results but never were able to go beyond that. Their followers gave no extra effort and denied the organization of their creative knowledge and energy. Let me list for you:

Profile of a Motivational Leader

Leaders That Motivate	Leaders That De-motivate
Generous with his time and talent	Holds back his praise and recognition
Erases all economic and social barriers	Holds those less fortunate in contempt
Focuses on others growth	Self-centered
Uplifts and encourages	Condemns and intimidates
Is trusted, respected and approachable	Is feared and avoided
Level headed and calm	Easily agitated
Exposes others to opportunities and development	Condemns and insults

Using Discipline

Dealing with people there are times when defined disciplinary action is necessary but must be used in good judgment. There has to be consequences for actions and discipline, but too much, or unnecessary discipline can demoralize people or the group very quickly. Over the years, I have adopted hat I have termed the "Physicians Rule" in determining to apply discipline and to what measure. Over the years I have been in a position where decisions had to be made regarding rule or policy violations.

One incident occurred while I was a Company Commander stationed in Panama. During a movement to the field a private dropped his rifle in the mud; his young Sergeant made him do excessive amounts of pushups and then made him stand exposed in the rain. When I found out about the incident that evening, I had the young sergeant come before me; he was facing serious charges for abuse and neglect. My First Sergeant recommended a Company Grade Article 15 which would destroy his career. After addressing the sergeant for some time I realized this was a young man had made a bad judgment but I also realized that I could not give him harsh punishment because I felt I and the senior staff had fallen short of our responsibility to provide meaningful training and mentoring to this young leader.

As a result I started conducting monthly leadership meetings with all officers and NCO's reviewing expectations of leadership and applying lessons learned.

I spent a great deal of time afterwards reflecting on my responsibility to help young emerging leaders to become better leaders in a military culture that demanded strict adherence to governance and rules. While in this state of contemplation, my mind raced back to when I was sixteen.

Use the Least Radical Surgery

When I was sixteen, I was involved in a particularly gruesome accident to my hand. In the emergency room, I was given medication to relieve my pain and was going in and out of consciousness.

I recall a young medical doctor coming to my side and telling me that they could not save my hand, it would have to be partially amputated. I was in no position to answer or respond. I just looked up into the face of the young doctor. His decision would have to be final. As the medical team gathered around, I could see the different devices used for the procedure.

A nurse stood over me and told me that I would not feel much pain, but there would be a slight burning sensation. Just as she said that, an older, more experienced doctor came in and stood by my side.

I recall him saying, "This is too radical, let me do something different, it will be better for him long term." I'm not sure what he meant or what he did, but I know today I am better off for his wisdom and experience. I am missing a portion of my finger, but I have had the benefit of my hand since that time.

Coming back to the employee waiting disciplinary action, I told the supervisor, "Let's use the least radical surgery to cure this problem." Another solution was taken, the employee was held accountable, his talents preserved, and his sense of fairness supported. Everyone came away better off.

"Use the least radical surgery to cure the problem"

Abraham Lincoln understood the damage that harshness and being inflexible had on people; he was guided by honesty, integrity, compassion and mercy. He did not do it because of pressure from those around him nor because of political impact. He was a leader of self-accountability and character who had no feelings of hate or malice. Those around him felt he was too kind, he was criticized by both military and civilian leaders for granting more pardons than any president before or since him had.

Lincoln's sons Willie and Tad were a product of their father's legacy and character; one day they were playing with a doll they had named Jack.

The boys had determined that Jack had fell asleep on guard duty, as result Jack was to be put to death. The boys went to their father and explained Jacks situation to which Lincoln declared on Executive Mansion stationary,

"The doll Jack is pardoned. By order of the President, signed A. Lincoln."

He signed Jacks pardon like he had signed all pardons.

What Fear Does to a Group

People tend to focus on basic issues, neglecting more complicated tasks

People are not willing to take risks

Creative energy is misdirected

People are satisfied with achieving short term results

Organizational goals and wellbeing are abandoned for personal security

Flexible ideas and policies transform into rigid policies

Communication tends to be filtered up. No one wants to talk to the boss, and when communications happens, it's calculated and risk-free

It creates bonding within small chat groups; none of which help to build the organization or add value for the leader

Chapter 9

Personality Disorders and Leadership

> "Nearly all men can stand adversity, but if you want to test a man's character, give him power."
>
> **Abraham Lincoln**

At every conference and speaking engagement on leadership, I am always asked the ultimate question.

"What are the main causes of ineffective leadership?"

While the answer is not simple nor can it be focused on one single element, most of it can be traced to selfishness and self-interests. Then it becomes even more complicated, because the definition of "ineffective" varies to a great degree.

In order to give a good understanding of ineffective, you must understand that often times, a leader with charismatic style who is popular within the top members of the organization, is usually, in reality a paradoxical hero; a person both loved and hated, idealized and scorned, a person not crazy, but thought to be by some of his followers. The leader usually display's a complex character and personality that is confusing and misdirected at times. This complexity of personality may be driven by unresolved struggles within the leader, and is what makes them volatile and ineffective.

Destructive Leadership Characteristics

Show anger when challenged.

People are quickly fired or leave (high turnover).

Fails to tap into ideas and talents of the group.

Covers up bad decisions by blaming others.

Gets results, but damages other's integrity and enthusiasm.

Ineffective leaders may have many successes, but eventually the damage created underneath the radar is revealed over time or through a catastrophic event. The best way to understand how this develops is to better understand the individual personalities of these ineffective leaders.

Individual personality inevitably causes one to encounter the essential character of that person, and their unique and individual identities. Often, people are said to have either strong or outgoing personalities based on behavior patterns they exhibit that are distinctive and consistent. Leaders may be described in terms such as, "driven", "intense", "direct", "focused" or "no-nonsense" . . . all terms which refer to some characteristic of that leader's personality.

For most leaders, these characteristics, as described by those around them, do not usually affect the group unless that characteristic is both persistent over time and across situations. For example, if your boss loses his temper one time in a year, that is not automatically a characteristic of that boss. But if the boss loses his temper every time his authority is challenged, that becomes a characteristic trait or "quirk," that can often times, be very destructive to the group and individuals. It is these personality characteristics, or "personality disorders," that make a leader ineffective.

Personality disorders are defined as, inflexible and enduring patterns of behavior that impair in some way, a leader's group functioning and limit maximum effectiveness. The disorders that the leader faces, becomes damaging or maladaptive if the leader is unable to modify the behavior when the situation or issue undergoes significant change calling for a different approach. The leader either cannot, or is not willing to adapt his or her behavior. Most leaders have only one or two characteristics of disorder, which do not significantly impair functioning as does a full-blown disorder. Only when personality becomes inflexible and maladaptive and causes significant function impairment or follower distress, does it become a personality disorder. The most common disorder for most leaders and bosses is a behavior disorder called **narcissism**.

The roots of the term "narcissism," originate from the classic Greek tragedy written by the Roman poet, Ovid Narcissus. Narcissism derives its name from Narcissus, and both derive from the Greek word nark "numb" from which we also get the word narcotic. Thus for the Greeks, Narcissus stood for vanity, callousness and insensitivity, as he was emotionally numb to the entreaties of those who fell in love with his beauty.

Today, we can see leaders with narcissism as being selfish, those who desire their own best interests, and not those of whom they serve. It is the root of most ineffective leadership, and being a behavior, can only be reformed by the leader themselves. This concept is particularly applicable to the relationship between those who, for example, become successful people in their own business, in the corporation, politics or other segments of society. In a sense, the narcissistic leader's view of themselves is justified by the views of others they surround themselves with. Among top organizational leaders and politicians, there is a degree of narcissism which may be considered an asset, especially among those who are "self-made," or who owe their success to those above them. The leader tends to regulate their own self-esteem through the manipulation of those under him or her. This is often manifested through conditioning of the group with anger, fear, reward & punishment, and even to the point of getting rid of those who do not acknowledge the leaders power and control, or who challenge the leader's authority.

Greek Legend of Narcissus

Narcissus was a spoiled, beautiful young man, who found himself loved by several maidens and would-be suitors through the forests of his homeland. As the son of the nymph Leriope, and the river-god Ceohissus, it is prophesized by the seer Tiresias that Narcissus would live to a ripe old age, provided that he never knew himself. A stubborn and prideful boy, Narcissus rejected all who would desire his love and attention.

Among those he rejected was the nymph Echo, who fell in love with Narcissus, but Narcissus cruelly rejected her. The nymphs prayed that Narcissus might love and feel the pains of rejection and not gain the thing that he loved. The prayer was heard and Narcissus was confronted with and then fell in love with, his own reflection while walking in the gardens of Echo.

Narcissus embraced the loved reflection, but it fled at his touch and returned again to fascinate him. His image apparently welcomed him; when he approached it, it approached him; when he stretched out his arms to it, it stretched out its arms to him. It seemed to want to be embraced, yet it fled when touched.

As the tragedy unfolds, Narcissus grieves for the image that he could see but not embrace ultimately realizing his passion was for the image of himself. Falling deeply in love with himself, he slowly wasted his days in awe of his reflection. After lying on the bank admiring his reflection, he became incapable of loving others.

As potential lovers approached him, seeking his attention and love, he quietly turned away and eventually died.

The narcissistic leader develops cracks in his or her effectiveness caused by the need for grandiosity. Grandiosity is observed by others as a pattern of self-importance, expectations of being recognized, preoccupation with fantasies of unlimited success or power, and a belief in one's uniqueness and sense of entitlement.

Clear examples surface every day, cases such as Col. Oliver North, who during the Contra Iran scandal, embezzled money orders and accepted unauthorized gifts in the form of a security system for his home. Ken Lay of Enron, who was convicted on charges of corruption and abuse of power.

Thomas Coughlin, and the former head of Wal-Mart's US retail operations was forced to resign from the board, after allegations that up to $500,000 was obtained from the company through unauthorised use of gift cards and false expense reports.

The list goes on, and will continue to grow as leaders get caught up in the network of power and sense of entitlement; a classical symptom of narcissism and selfishness.

Grandiosity—"I am better than you."

Grandiosity is a symptom of bad leadership, it is the attitude that I am better than you and can cripple a leader when he or she really begins to believe there ultimate superiority. There are eight components of grandiosity found in leaders with personality quirks associated with narcissism. Many leaders who are vulnerable to narcissism also have tendencies to go into unreasonable rages, followed by embarrassment and shame, having very little control at stopping or limiting them. These rages are often triggered or occur in response to perceived slights, rebuffs, and rejections, and thus, are clearly related to their need for control and power.

The leader views him or her, as being attacked, and tends to take issues personal. This may be a response to defend their status and position of power. When in actuality, the perceived attacks are simply a healthy exchange of opinions and ideas that, under normal leadership, is encouraged and supported.

8 Characteristics of Grandiosity

Exaggerates talents, capacity, and achievements in an unrealistic way

Believes in their own invulnerability or do not recognize their limitations.

Believes they do not need other people.

Regards themselves as unique or special compared to others.

Regards themselves as generally superior to others.

Self-cantered—disregarding other's ideas and opinions.

Appears or behaves in a boastful way.

Arrogant and haughty. They are viewed as snobbish, better than others, and patronizing towards others.

I have witnessed narcissistic leaders go into an emotional stage similar to pouting, visibly withdrawing their emotional support, stopping meaningful engagement, and essentially shutting others out. It is the grandiose qualities of the leader that under normal circumstances, suffice to protect the ego of these leaders. But when internal experiences become more than the person's protective barriers can handle, the result is usually an almost uncontrollable rage/child-like cycle. I have also noticed that in these leaders, there is a correlation between education and the intensity of the cycle. Most leaders who fall into these rages may be limited in education, lack the ability to understand or develop protective barriers, and lack an understanding of how their behaviour impacts others.

How Did They Get In Position of Leadership?

Most managers and leaders you know in your organization have been promoted because they demonstrated ambition and were able to control or manage small volumes of processes or people. As those managers move up into the organization they are given more power and authority. As a result, personalities can be transformed and style changed, as their egos are fed by power. As people climb higher up this power structure, more time is spent by the leader on his or her ego functions and less on the needs of the organization and others. So it's not surprising when you hear the phrase, "power corrupts"; it may be true.

It is important to realize that we all have narcissistic tendencies, but it is a matter of recognizing and controlling them and not letting them create an unhealthy management style.

Seven Signs of Narcissistic Leaders

Overly concerned with "how they look".

Rigid.

Preoccupied with details.

Demonstrates an unusual need for control.

Demonstrates an excessive devotion to work and productivity.

Does not trust others and lacks empathy.

Lacks the ability to develop personal relationships.

The problem with narcissism is that it creates a paranoia behavior, making it difficult for these managers and leaders to be accessible to their employees, because they tend to loose trust in everyone except a small hand-picked group of associates. It is usually disguised by being too busy with a full schedule that does not allow time for reflecting and evaluating. They spend time micro-managing and controlling every process.

Self-centeredness, distrust of their employees, and their need for absolute control, cause these leaders to be perceived as superficial and fake, and in turn the leaders develop a suspicious view of their workers. They focus too much on the outward person; their problems, mistakes, and faults, failing to recognize their individual talents and potential. Narcissistic leaders tend to surround themselves with managers and leaders who have the similar quality of exploiting others, and who will support their views and opinions even when they know their advice and views are wrong.

The tragedy of narcissist leaders is that over time, a culture within the group or organization begins to emerge characterized by mistrust; change is controlled, spontaneous ideas and creativity are discouraged. The top becomes filled with "yes" men, who limit their contribution to what the leader wants to hear by filtering information up to the top. Another damaging effect to the followers and organization is the emotional toll it takes on the team, as their personal values are ignored or in some cases attacked. Employees become neglected when there is no recognition, reward, or meaningful communication. Employees become less committed, hostile towards the organization and eventually find other work. Teams cannot survive since there is no support for the manager or his ideas. Most effective leaders realize that building trust requires them to positively drive their people's moods and performance. They understand that fear and anger are a mobilizing force; but is very short term. Narcissist leaders fail to comprehend these principles as an aid for motivation and team building. They fail to mobilize the talents and commitment of the people.

The most concerning and dangerous characteristic of narcissistic leaders, is that they seldom give up power; they may delegate simple tasks, but never the power. They will impose strict rules and guidelines; impose fuzzy boundaries where cohesion is impossible to attain. They refuse responsibility; they are the declared experts, making others feel inferior and guilty. Every failure is criticized and announced so that a fear develops for failure. It is in these organizations that lying and falsification of numbers and information occurs, because of the perceived reprisals.

Narcissistic leaders are highly manipulative, their actions and motives do not spring from a deep sense of caring for others, but from a need to use them to achieve their own goals and satisfy their own needs. These leaders are not focused on the long term effect of their actions, but rush to solve problems by seeking to stop the present pain, and thereby create greater difficulty and pain later on.

Do not confuse Narcissism with Quirkiness or Ambition

Narcissism can be confused with quirks, which are magnified character traits. Quirks usually do not have the same long term impact that narcissist leaders have on others. Quirks are magnified behavior preferences, such as a boss who demands a clean desk as a sign of organization, or a boss who becomes irritated when people are late for a meeting; neither have an impact on the bottom line or on the organization, it is simply irritating to the leader. A quirk becomes a disorder when it impacts the talent pool or the ability of the organization to function. Quirkiness is a prelude to Narcissism but is not as serious and often does not distract from the leader's effectiveness.

Ambition unlike quirkiness is not a bad trait, and may be absolutely necessary for effective leadership. Ambition is best described as energy and determination, good when balanced and dangerous unbalanced. People without energy are those who say, "One day I will be in a better position," but then, never get there. It is critical for leaders to have the ability to stay focused and on task, through completion. Finally, if you want to determine if your ambition is unbalanced, ask yourself this question. Am I driven to succeed at the expense of others, or am I driven to succeed collectively, that all may benefit? Ambition directed toward the benefit of others is an important quality for us all to obtain.

Why It's Important to Understand Personality Disorders

Personality disorders and leadership is essential for us to understand, because of the influence of character on organizations and the people who are influenced by them. If we know that healthy leaders can profoundly have positive influence of organizational results and people, then unhealthy leadership has an equal impact and affects with negative impact and influence. Leaders have impact upon the employees and for this reason, the character and behavior of a leader should be of interest to the organizational leaders. Logic would suggest that the pathology of the organization is a result of the pathology of its leaders.

A certain amount of ego and narcissism are necessary, and may be needed to function as a leader; however, the stronger the narcissist tendency, the more vulnerable the leader becomes to over stimulation as result of power and sense to protect self. These leaders develop the need for power and prestige, and assume positions of authority and leadership. Individuals with such characteristics are found rather frequently in top leadership positions. It is the responsibility of investors and top leaders, to insure that these leaders' motives are understood and that those who are motivated for power and prestige are prevented from reaching the bowels of the organization.

Labeling bad bosses as having personality disorders is not fair or always accurate but the fact is there are some bosses/leaders, which are a pleasure to work for. They are kind, helpful, honest, benevolent, and motivating. Then there are those who are abrupt, blunt, direct, intense, and cold-hearted. They lack the ability to motivate and inspire. We avoid them, minimize communications with them and most of all do not enjoy being around them. The first type boss arouses in us an eagerness to participate, engage and be at work. The other boss creates in us a fear, avoidance, even hostility.

Chapter 10

Character and Courage

> **"Nearly all men can stand adversity, but if you want to test a man's character, give him power."**
>
> **Abraham Lincoln**

The decisions we make as leaders and the way we behave are what ultimately shape our character. Charles A. Hall aptly described that process in these lines:

"We sow our thoughts, and we reap our actions; we sow our actions, and we reap our habits; we sow our habits, and we reap our characters; we sow our characters, and we reap our destiny"

Most leaders with a "dark side", often times lack character that is essential for healthy and effective leadership.

Character is a person's moral and ethical qualities that helps determine what is right and gives a leader motivation to do what is appropriate, regardless of the circumstances or the consequences. An informed ethical conscience consistent with the Organizations Values strengthens leaders to make the right choices when faced with tough issues. Since leaders seek to do what is right and inspire others to do the same, they must embody these values.

There is a direct connection between the leader's character and his actions. Character, discipline, and good judgment allow front line leaders to make decisions and take actions that are admirable to the followers as well as in their best interest. Character is essential to successful leadership. It determines who people are and how they act. It helps determine right from wrong and choose what is right.

Front line leaders enter the work force with personal values developed in childhood and nurtured over many years of personal experience. When agreeing to an employment contract, one also agrees to live and act by a new set of values—The Organizations Values. The Organizations Values consist of the principles, standards, and qualities considered essential for successful the organization and its leaders. They are fundamental to helping the workforce make the right decision in any business situation.

Character Development

People join the organization as members of a new group or teams with their character, pre-shaped by their background, beliefs, education, and experience. A Leader's job would be simpler if merely checking the team member's personal values against the Organizations Values and developing a simple plan to align them. Reality is much different. Becoming a person of character and a leader of character is a career long process involving day-to-day experience, education, self-development, developmental counseling, coaching, and mentoring. While individuals are responsible for their own character development, leaders are responsible for encouraging, supporting, and assessing the efforts of their people. Leaders of character can develop only through continual study, reflection, experience, and feedback. Leaders hold themselves and followers to the highest standards. The standards and values then spread throughout the team, or unit and ultimately throughout the culture of the entire organization.

Doing the right thing is good. Doing the right thing for the right reason and with the right goal is better. People of character must possess the desire to act ethically in all situations. One of the leader's primary responsibilities is to maintain an ethical climate that supports development of such character. When an organization's ethical climate nurtures ethical behavior, people will, over time, think, feel, and act ethically. They will internalize the aspects of sound character.

Character and Beliefs

Beliefs matter because they help people understand their experiences. Those experiences provide a start point for what to do in everyday situations. Beliefs are convictions people hold as true. Values are deep-seated personal beliefs that shape a person's behavior. Values and beliefs are central to character.

Leaders should recognize the role beliefs play in preparing followers for assignments and work within the group. Employees often work against challenging and work requirements often times under tremendous pressures when they are convinced of the beliefs for which they are asked to perform. Commitment to such beliefs as fairness, equity, and cared for can be essential ingredients in creating and sustaining commitment and performance.

Beliefs derive from upbringing, culture, religious backgrounds, and traditions. As a result, different moral beliefs have, and will, continue to be shaped by diverse religious and philosophical traditions.

Character and Ethics

Adhering to the principles that Organizational Values embody is essential to upholding high ethical standards of behavior. Unethical behavior quickly destroys organizational morale and cohesion—it undermines the trust and confidence essential to teamwork and mission accomplishment. Consistently doing the right thing forges strong character in individuals and expands to create a culture of trust throughout the organization.

Ethics are concerned with how a person should behave. Values represent the beliefs that a person has. The translation from desirable ethics to internal values to actual behavior involves choices. Keep in mind that ethical reasoning is very complex in practice. The process to resolve ethical dilemmas involves critical thinking based on the Organizational Values. No formula will work every time. By embracing the Organization Values to govern personal actions, understanding standards and guidelines, learning from experiences, and applying multiple perspectives of ethics, leaders will be prepared to face tough calls in life.

Warrant Officer Thompson at My Lai, Vietnam

On 16 March 1968, WO1 Hugh C. Thompson, Jr. and his two-man helicopter crew were on a reconnaissance mission over the village of My Lai, Republic of Vietnam.

WO1 Thompson watched in horror as he saw an American Soldier shoot an injured Vietnamese child. Minutes later, he observed more Soldiers advancing on a number of civilians in a ditch. Suspecting possible reprisal shootings, WO1 Thompson landed his helicopter and questioned a young officer about what was happening. Told that the ground combat action was none of his business, WO1 Thompson took off and continued to circle the embattled area.

When it became apparent to Thompson that the American troops had now begun firing on more unarmed civilians, he landed his helicopter between the Soldiers and a group of ten villagers headed towards a homemade bomb shelter. Thompson ordered his gunner to train his weapon on the approaching Soldiers and to fire if necessary. Then he personally coaxed the civilians out of the shelter and airlifted them to safety.

WO1 Thompson's immediate radio reports about what was happening triggered a cease-fire order that ultimately saved the lives of many more villagers.

Thompson's willingness to place himself in physical danger to do the ethically and morally right.

Thompson's choices prevented further atrocities on the ground and demonstrated that duty conscious Americans ultimately enforce moral standards of decency. Our employees and followers must have the personal and moral courage to block criminal behavior and to protect their fellow workers.

Leaders must consistently focus on shaping ethics-based organizational climates in which followers and organizations can achieve their full potential. To reach their goal, leaders can use tools such as the Ethical Climate Assessment Survey's or ask HR to assess ethical aspects of their own character and actions, the workplace, and the external environment. Once they have done a climate assessment, leaders prepare and follow a plan of action. The plan of action focuses on solving ethical problems within the leader's span of influence, while the higher corporate group is informed of ethical problems that cannot be changed at the front line level.

Ethical Reasoning

To be an ethical leader requires more than knowing the Organizational values. Leaders must be able to apply them to find moral solutions to diverse problems. Ethical reasoning occurs both as an informal process natural to thinking and as an integral part of the formal problem solving model. Ethical considerations occur naturally during all steps of the formal process from identifying the problem through making and implementing the decision. The model specifically states that ethics are explicit considerations when selecting screening criteria, when conducting analysis, and during the comparison of possible solutions.

Ethical choices may be between right and wrong, shades of gray, or two rights. Some problems center on an ethical dilemma requiring special consideration of what is most ethical. Leaders use multiple perspectives to think about an ethical problem, applying all three perspectives to determine the most ethical choice. One perspective comes from the view that desirable virtues such as courage, justice, and benevolence define ethical outcomes. A second perspective comes from the set of agreed-upon values or rules, such as the Organizational Values or rights established by the legal courts. A third perspective bases the consequences of the decision on whatever produces the greatest good for the greatest number is most favorable.

Leaders are expected do the right things for the right reasons all the time. That is why followers count on their leaders to be more than just skilled and proficient. They rely on them to make good decisions that are also ethical. Determining what is right and ethical can be a difficult task. Ethical dilemmas are nothing new for leaders. Although it often seems critical to gain timely and valuable intelligence from insurgent detainees or enemy prisoners, what measures are appropriate to obtain vital information from the enemy that could save lives? Vaguely understood instructions from higher management could present one reason why followers sometimes push the limits past the framework of what is legal, believing they are doing their duty. Nothing could be more dangerous from an ethical perspective, and nothing could do more harm to the reputation of the organization and its existence. If legal limits are clearly in question, the Organizations Values bind everyone involved, regardless of rank, to do something about it. Leaders have a responsibility and the duty to research relevant orders, rules, and regulations and to demand clarification of orders that could lead to criminal misinterpretation or abuse. Ultimately, leaders must accept the consequences of their actions.

Ethical Directives

Making the right choice and acting on it when faced with an ethical question can be difficult. Sometimes it means standing firm and disagreeing with the boss on ethical grounds. These occasions test character. Situations in which a leader thinks an illegal order is issued can be the most difficult.

Under normal circumstances, a leader executes a superior leader's decision with energy and enthusiasm. The only exception would be illegal directive, which a leader has a duty to disobey. If a follower perceives that a directive is illegal, that follower should be sure the details of the order and its original intent are fully understood. The follower should seek immediate clarification from the person who gave it before proceeding.

If the question is more complex, seek legal counsel. If it requires an immediate decision, as may happen in tough business decisions, make the best judgment possible based on the Organization Values, personal experience, critical thinking, and previous study and reflection. There is a risk when a leader disobeys what may be an illegal request or directive, and it may be the most difficult decision that a leader ever makes. Nonetheless, that is what competent, confident, and ethical leaders should do.

The Organizational Values firmly bind all members into a fellowship dedicated to serve the organization. They apply to everyone, in every situation, anywhere in the Organization. The trust members have for each other and the trust of the stakeholders, all depend on how well a leader embodies the Organization Values.

Five values for effective leadership

Respect

Selfless service.

Integrity.

Personal moral courage.

Loyalty

Loyalty

The loyalty of subordinates is a gift given when a leader deserves it. Leaders earn subordinates' loyalty by training them well, treating them fairly, and living the organizational values. Leaders who are loyal to their followers never let them be misused or abused. Followers who believe in their leaders will stand with them no matter how difficult the situation.

Loyalty and trust are extremely important ingredients for the successful day-to-day operations of all organizations. To create strong organizations and tight-knit teams, all team members must embrace loyalty—supervisors, subordinates, peers, contractors and followers.

Respect

Respect for the individual is the basis for the rule of law—the very essence of what the organization stands for. Respect means treating others as they should be treated. This value reiterates that people are the most precious resource and that one is bound to treat others with dignity and respect.

Over the course of history, our workforce has become more culturally diverse, requiring leaders to deal with people from a wider range of ethnic, racial, and religious backgrounds. A leader should prevent misunderstandings arising from cultural differences. Actively seeking to learn about people whose culture is different can help to do this. Being sensitive to other cultures will aid in mentoring, coaching, and counseling subordinates. This demonstrates respect when seeking to understand their background, see things from their perspective, and appreciate what is important to them.

Leaders should consistently foster a climate in which everyone is treated with dignity and respect, regardless of race, gender, creed, or religious belief. Fostering a balanced and dignified work climate begins with a leader's personal example. How a leader lives the organizational values shows followers how they should behave. Teaching values is one of a leader's most important responsibilities. It helps create a common understanding of expected standards.

> **The discipline which makes the soldiers of a free country reliable in battle is not to be gained by harsh or tyrannical treatment. On the contrary, such treatment is far more likely to destroy than to make an army.**
>
> **It is possible to impart instruction and to give commands in such manner and such a tone of voice to inspire in the soldier no feeling but an intense desire to obey, while the opposite manner and tone of voice cannot fail to excite strong resentment and a desire to disobey.**
>
> **The one mode or the other of dealing with subordinates springs from a corresponding spirit in the breast of the commander.**

> **He who feels the respect which is due to others cannot fail to inspire in them regard for himself, while he who feels, and hence manifests, disrespect toward others, especially his inferiors, cannot fail to inspire hatred against himself.**
>
> Major General John M. Schofield
> 11 August 1879

Selfless Service

Selfless service means doing what is right for the employees and the organization. While the needs of the organization should come first, it does not imply family or self-neglect. To the contrary, such neglect weakens a leader and can cause the organization more harm than good.

Ambition can be compatible with selfless service, as long as the leader treats his people fairly and gives them the credit they deserve. The leader knows that the organization cannot function except as a team. For a team to excel, the individual must give up Self-interest for the good of the whole.

Integrity

Leaders of integrity consistently act according to clear principles, not just what works now. The organization relies on leaders of integrity who possess high moral standards and who are honest in word and deed. Leaders are honest to others by not presenting themselves or their actions as anything other than what they are, remaining committed to the truth.

Here is how a leader stands for the truth: if an assignment cannot be accomplished, the leader's integrity requires him to inform his manager. If the unit's organizations' performance rate is truly 70 percent, despite the senior managers required standard of 90 percent, a leader of integrity will not instruct subordinates to adjust numbers. It is the leader's duty to report the truth and develop solutions to meet the standard with honor and integrity. Identifying the underlying maintenance issues and raising the quality bar could ultimately save money and the integrity of the followers.

If leaders inadvertently pass on bad information, they should correct it as soon as they discover the error. Leaders of integrity do the right thing not because it is convenient or because they have no other choice. They choose the path of truth because their character permits nothing less.

Serving with integrity encompasses more than one component. However, these components are dependent on whether the leader inherently understands right versus wrong. Assuming the leader can make the distinction, a leader should always be able to separate right from wrong in every situation. Just as important, that leader should do what is right, even at personal cost.

Leaders cannot hide what they do, but must carefully decide how to act. Leaders are always on display. To instill Values in others, leaders must demonstrate them personally. Personal values may extend beyond the Organizational Values, to include such things as political, cultural, or religious beliefs. However, as a leader and a person of integrity, these values should reinforce, not contradict, the Organizational Values.

Conflicts between personal and Organizational Values should be resolved before a leader becomes a morally complete leader. If in doubt, a leader may consult a mentor with respected values and judgment.

Moral Courage

Physical courage requires overcoming fears of bodily harm and doing one's duty. It triggers bravery that allows a person to take risks in spite of the fear of harm or even death. Most leaders in business will not need to experience nor demonstrate physical courage but they will nearly always be challenged with moral courage.

Moral courage is the willingness to stand firm on values, principles, and convictions. It enables all leaders to stand up for what they believe is right, regardless of the consequences. Leaders, who take full responsibility for their decisions and actions, even when things go wrong, display moral courage.

Moral courage also expresses itself as candor. Candor means being frank, honest, and sincere with others. It requires steering clear of bias, prejudice, or malice even when it is uncomfortable or may seem better to keep quiet.

One can observe candor when a supervisor calmly explains to his boss that an employee should receive a lower-level reprimand, although the boss insists on a harsher action to include termination. Likewise, a candid leader respectfully points out a boss might be overreacting for ordering a harsh revision of local policy that may affect the entire work group, when only one line or unit actually failed a quality control inspection. Trust relationships between leaders and subordinates rely on candor. Without it, subordinates will not know if they have met the standard and leaders will not know what is going on in their organization.

Courage; it is an absolute for leaders. In fact, I would suggest that without courage, you cannot be an effective leader at home, the workplace, or in society in general. It is the fabric that good leaders are cut from and allows for bold decisions and acts. There are two types of courage that are essential for effective leadership.

Can courage be learned? It can, in the sense that the development of deep devotion to a cause galvanizes a person to act on behalf of that cause. This type of fundamental belief in the value of the mission is essential to the cultivation of courage, whether it be physical or moral.

Only a profound conviction that there is a good greater than self can spark a person to risk everything for others. Self-sacrifice, and the courage to take that chance, is the antithesis of "me-generation" philosophy. When the lives or liberties of others are valued more highly than one's own life, then true courage can provide the fuel for remarkable accomplishments.

Two Faces of Courage—Physical and Moral

Leaders must understand what courage is. There are different kinds of courage—physical courage and moral courage.

Physical Courage. When a sense of mission becomes powerful enough to motivate people to action, even in the face of personal danger or certain death that is physical courage. To be courageous one need not be fearless; it is natural and good to be afraid when confronted with real risks. But so long as that fear does not paralyze, there is courage at work.

Raoul Wallenberg's story as told latter in this chapter, demonstrates physical courage, as he ignored armed soldiers and even flying bullets to continue his rescue operations. He had the audacity to threaten high-ranking Nazi officers, who had proved their willingness to murder innocent civilians, let alone troublesome opponents, under conditions where they easily could have killed him. Although in constant fear for his life, he pressed on, risking and ultimately sacrificing himself for his mission.

Moral Courage, which is defined by one's unwavering belief and values of right and wrong and as defined by personal commitment. It is my experience however, that leaders with moral courage, (that is, one who is true to himself), also have physical courage. The great Shakespeare, in his play, Hamlet, has his character Polonius, instruct his son on many aspects of his conduct. And he concludes a rather long statement with these words: ***"To thine own self be true"***

The Raoul Wallenberg Story of Courage

No story better illustrates courage than Raoul Wallenberg. The story is best told by an excerpt from, The Journal of Leadership Studies, 1997, Vol. 4, No. 3, authored by John Kunich and Richard Lestaer.

Raoul Wallenberg was a Swedish diplomat who went to Budapest in 1944 to intervene on behalf of Hungary's 700,000 Jews, who were being deported by the Nazis to extermination camps.

During the waning months of World War II, the Allies were desperate for ways to stop Hitler's slaughter of innocent civilians in Eastern Europe. Even as the prospects for an Axis military victory dimmed, the Nazis grew more determined to complete the "final solution." Death camps operated at maximum capacity in a feverish effort to rid Europe of Jews, and other target groups. Until a complete military triumph could be secured, the Allies were powerless to halt the genocide raging on behind enemy lines. Therefore, a volunteer was sought—someone who could go where allied tanks and aircraft could not, and disrupt the insidious, Nazi death machine.

No one could have been a less obvious choice for this mission than Raoul Wallenberg. Wallenberg was 32 years old in 1944, a wealthy, upper-class Swede from a prominent, well-respected family. Sweden's neutrality in the war was only one in a long series of ready-made excuses life had handed young Wallenberg, had he wanted to use them to refuse the rescue mission. He was not Jewish, he was rich, he was well-connected politically, he was in line to take the helm of the vast Wallenberg financial empire, and he had everything to lose and nothing to gain by accepting this challenge.

Wallenberg was recommended for this endeavor by Koloman Lauer, a business partner who was involved with the new War Refugee Board. Lauer felt that Raoul possessed the proper combination of dedication, skill, and courage, despite his youth and inexperience, and that his family name would afford him some protection. Wallenberg proved eager to serve, but he boldly demanded and was granted, a great deal of latitude in the methods he would use.

When he learned that Adolf Eichmann was transporting roughly ten to twelve thousand Jews to the gas chambers each day, Wallenberg hastily prepared to travel to Budapest. His "cover" was that of a diplomat, with the official title of First Secretary of the Swedish Legation. He conceived a plan whereby false Swedish passports (Schutzpasse) would be created and used to give potential victims safe passage out of Nazi-controlled territory. In conjunction with this, a series of safe-`houses would be established within Hungary, in the guise of official Swedish legation buildings under diplomatic protection. With this scheme still forming in his mind, "Swedish diplomat" Wallenberg, entered Hungary at the request of the United States War Refugee Board, and his own government on July 6th, 1944, with the mission of saving as many of Hungary's Jews as possible from Nazi liquidation.

He designed the fake passports himself. They were masterpieces, the type of formal, official-appearing pomp which was so impressive to the Nazis. Wallenberg, though young, had traveled and studied extensively abroad, both in the United States (where he attended the University of Michigan as a student of architecture) and in Europe, and he knew how to deal with people and get things done. He worked hard at understanding enemies as well as allies, to know what motivated them; what they admired, what they feared, what they respected. He correctly concluded that the Nazis and Hungarian fascists (Arrow Cross) with whom he would be dealing responded best to absolute authority and official status. He used this principle in fashioning his passports as well as in his personal encounters with the enemy.

Wallenberg began with forty important contacts in Budapest, and quickly cultivated others who were willing to help. It is estimated that under Wallenberg's leadership he and his associates distributed Swedish passports to twenty thousand of Budapest's Jews and protected thirteen thousand more in safe houses, which he rented and over which flew the Swedish flag. However, Eichmann continued to pursue his own mission with fanatical, zealous devotion, and the death camps roared around the clock. Trains packed with people, crammed eighty to a cattle car with nothing but a little water and a bucket for waste, constantly made the four-day journey from Budapest to Auschwitz and back again. The Hungarian countryside was already devoid of Jews, and the situation in the last remaining urban enclaves was critical. And so, Wallenberg himself plunged into the midst of the struggle.

Sandor Ardai was sent by the underground to drive for Wallenberg. Ardai later told of one occasion when Wallenberg intercepted a trainload of prisoners about to leave for Auschwitz. Wallenberg swept past the SS officer who ordered him to depart. In Ardai's words:

"Then he climbed up on the roof of the train and began handing in protective passes through the doors which were not yet sealed. He ignored orders from the Germans for him to get down. Then the Arrow Cross men began shooting and shouting at him to go away. He ignored them and calmly continued handing out passports to the hands that were reaching out for them. I believe the Arrow Cross men deliberately aimed over his head, as not one shot hit him, which would have been impossible otherwise. I think they did this because they were so impressed by his courage. After Wallenberg had handed over the last of the passports, he ordered all those who had one to leave the train and walk to the caravan of cars parked nearby, all marked in Swedish colors. I don't remember exactly how many,

but he saved dozens off that train, and the Germans and Arrow Cross were so dumbfounded they let him get away with it!" (Bierman 91)

As the war situation deteriorated for the Germans, Eichmann diverted trains from the death camp routes for more direct use in supplying troops. But all this meant for his victims was that they now had to walk to their destruction. In November, 1944, Eichmann ordered the 125-mile death marches, and the raw elements soon combined with deprivation of food and sleep, turned the roadside from Budapest to the camps, into one massive graveyard. Wallenberg made frequent visits to the stopping areas to do what he could.

In one instance, Wallenberg announced his arrival with all the authority he could muster, and then, "You there!"

The Swede pointed to an astonished man, waiting for his turn to be handed over to the executioner.

"Give me your Swedish passport and get in that line," he barked. "And you get behind him. I know I issued you a passport."

Wallenberg continued, moving fast, talking loud; hoping the authority in his voice would somehow rub off on these defeated people . . . The Jews finally caught on. They started groping in pockets for bits of identification. A driver's license or birth certificate seemed to do the trick. The Swede was grabbing them so fast; the Nazis, who couldn't read Hungarian anyway, didn't seem to be checking. Faster, Wallenberg's eyes urged them, faster, before the game is up. In minutes he had several hundred people in his convoy. International Red Cross trucks arrived there at Wallenberg's behest, and the Jews clambered on . . . Wallenberg jumped into his own car.

He leaned out of the car window and whispered, "I am sorry," to the people he was leaving behind. "I am trying to take the youngest ones first," he explained, "I want to save a nation."

This type of action worked many times. Wallenberg and his aides would encounter a death march, and, while Raoul shouted orders for all those with Swedish protective passports to raise their hands, his assistants ran up and down the prisoners' ranks, telling them to raise their hands whether or not they had a document. Wallenberg "then claimed custody of all who had raised their hands and such was his bearing, that none of the Hungarian guards opposed him. The extraordinary thing was the "absolute, convincing power of his behavior," according to Joni Moser.

Wallenberg indirectly helped many who never even saw his face, because as his deeds were talked about, they inspired hope, courage, and action in many people who otherwise felt powerless to escape destruction. He became a symbol of good in a part of the world dominated by evil, and a reminder of the hidden strengths within each human spirit.

Tommy Lapid was thirteen years old in 1944, when he was one of nine hundred people crowded fifteen or twenty to a room in one of the Swedish safe houses. His account illustrates not only vintage Wallenberg tactics, but also how Wallenberg epitomized hope and righteousness, and how his influence extended throughout the land as a beacon to those engulfed in the darkness of despair.

"One morning, a group of these Hungarian Fascists came into the house and said that all the able-bodied women must go with them. We knew what this meant. My mother kissed me and I cried and she cried. We knew we were parting forever and she left me there, an orphan to all intents and purposes. Then, two or three hours later, to my amazement, my mother returned with the other women. It seemed like a mirage, a miracle. My mother was there—she was alive and she was hugging me and kissing me, and she said one word, *"Wallenberg."* I knew who she meant, because Wallenberg was a legend among the Jews. In the complete and total hell in which we lived, there was a savior-angel somewhere, moving around. After she had composed herself, my mother told me that they were being taken to the river when a car arrived and out stepped Wallenberg—and they knew immediately who it was, because there was only one such person in the world. He went up to the Arrow Cross leader and protested that the women were under his protection. They argued with him, but he must have had incredible charisma or some great personal authority, because there was absolutely nothing behind him, no one to back him up. He stood out there in the street, probably feeling like the loneliest man in the world, trying to pretend there was

something or someone behind him. They could have shot him then and there in the street and nobody would have known about it. Instead, they relented and let the women go."

Virtually alone in the middle of enemy territory, outnumbered and outgunned beyond belief, Wallenberg worked miracles on a daily basis. His weapons were courage, self-confidence, ingenuity, understanding of his adversaries, and the ability to inspire others to achieve the goals he set. His leadership was always in evidence. The Nazis and Arrow Cross did not know how to deal with such a man. Here was someone thickly cloaked in apparent authority, but utterly devoid of actual political or military power. Here was a man who was everything they wished they could be in terms of personal strength of character, except for the fact that he was their polar opposite in purpose.

It is impossible to calculate precisely how many people Raoul Wallenberg directly or indirectly saved from certain death. Some estimate the number saved as close to one hundred thousand, and countless more may have survived, in part because of the hope and determination they derived from his leadership and example. (House of Representatives Report, Ninety-Sixth Congress, 2-3). Additionally, he inspired other neutral embassies and the International Red Cross office in Budapest, to join in his efforts to protect the Jews. But the desperate days just prior to the Soviet occupation of Budapest, presented Wallenberg with his greatest challenge and most astonishing triumph.

Eichmann planned to finish the extermination of the remaining one hundred thousand Budapest Jews, in one enormous massacre; if there was no time to ship them to the death camps, he would let their own neighborhoods become their slaughterhouses. To cheat the Allies out of at least part of their victory, he would order some five hundred SS men, and a large number of Arrow Cross, to ring the ghetto and murder the Jews right there. Wallenberg learned of this plot through his network of contacts and tried to intimidate some lower-ranking authorities into backing down, but with the Soviets on their doorsteps, many ceased to care what happened to them. His only hope, and the only hope for the 100,000 surviving Jews, was the overall commander of the SS troops, General August Schmidthuber.

Wallenberg sent a message to Schmidthuber that, if the massacre took place, he would ensure Schmidthuber was held personally responsible and would see him hanged as a war criminal. The bluff worked. The slaughter was called off, and the city fell out of Nazi hands soon thereafter when the Soviet troops rolled in. Thus, tens of thousands were saved in this one incident alone.

But, while peace came to Europe, Wallenberg's fate took a very different path. He vanished, and the whole truth of what happened to him has not been revealed even to this day. From various sources, though, the following seems to have occurred.

The Soviets took Wallenberg into custody when they occupied Budapest, probably because they suspected him of being an anti-Soviet spy. For a decade, they denied any involvement in Wallenberg's disappearance. Then they admitted having incarcerated him, but claimed he died in prison of a heart attack in 1947, when he would have been 35 years old. Since then, however, many people who have served time in Soviet prison have reported seeing Wallenberg, conversing with him, or communicating with him through tap codes. Others have heard of him and his presence in the prisons, but had no direct contact. The Soviets have denied the accuracy of all of these reports and have never deviated from their official position.

In 1989, Soviet officials met with members of Wallenberg's family and turned over some of his personal effects. Reportedly, a genuine investigation was launched in an effort to determine the truth. Whether the years and the prisons will ever yield up their secrets remains to be seen.

Adolf Eichmann, summarized his feelings for Raoul Wallenberg in this way:

> **"There is much we all can learn from Raoul Wallenberg's leadership. His courage came from caring for others, hoping for their success and not his own. He demonstrated both moral and physical courage because he had a choice, he was not forced into the situation; he chose to be a part of it."**
>
> *Adolf Eichmann*

As a leader, Wallenberg was out front, not in the corporate offices or behind the wealth of his family. He showed courage and sincerity. He responded to an obvious need with imagination and creativity. He would not want today's generation to feel sorry for him, I am sure he knew, he understood what was involved and he fully accepted the consequences.

Finally, he knew himself. He had a grasp of his talents and weaknesses and how they fit in with his purpose and goals. Thus, what he could not possibly have accomplished through military force or physical violence, he did through bravado, intimidation, and illusion. Any other tactics would have met with crushing defeat. This is not to imply that leaders should always behave in this manner. It simply suggests that these strategies employed by Wallenberg, were essential to fulfill his objective under the most extraordinary of conditions, and that they were chosen with full comprehension of the alternatives and their consequences. But most importantly, his motive was pure, it was not for selfish gratification and gain; it was because he saw the Jews as his friends.

Becoming a mature leader means first becoming yourself, learning who you are and what you stand for. Implicit in this notion is the theory of self-discovery, getting in touch with oneself. Wallenberg teaches us that to grow as a leader involves reflecting on oneself, putting values in perspective, thinking about the task to be accomplished, and influencing and motivating others to get the job done.

Wallenberg's work in Hungary is a testimony that leaders are foot soldiers who battle for the ideals in which they believe, and that leadership has far less to do with using other people than with serving other people.

Selfless service is the key to successful leadership, which in turn can result in meaningful accomplishments. Raoul Wallenberg found himself and the meaning of his life, by losing it in the service of others.

The process of learning about oneself and others, on an in-depth level, requires hard work. It is not something that can be gained solely from book study. It evolves best through personal introspection, human interaction and feedback, and through life experiences, observations, and analysis.

It involves large quantities of common sense and realistic perspective. But its yield is high; it pays big dividends to those leaders who spend the time and make the extra effort to go beneath the surface, to discover what makes a person tick; because life and its activities are all part of the human experience. Bottom line; it is all a matter of people, and the leader who understands people, understands leadership.

Wallenberg's work in Hungary demonstrates that effective leadership is neither neutral nor sterile. It is deeply emotional, and leaders cannot set aside the individual and their needs, and have a deeply felt belief in the worth of those who follow them; not merely a casual sense of, "it's only a job". Total commitment comes only from total conviction that the people we serve are significant to the organization.

Leaders are not afraid to do the unexpected

Throughout his entire experience in Hungary, in all that he did, Wallenberg had the daring to accept himself as a bundle of possibilities. He boldly undertook the game of making the most of his best. Wallenberg instructs us that the leader is not a superman, but simply a fully functioning human being.

Successful leaders are aware of their possibilities and do not let self-ambition to please others or to build up one's own pride, take over. Such leaders become afraid to take risks and are afraid to do the unexpected.

Erich Fromm said that the pity in life today is that most of us die before we are fully born. Leaders such as Wallenberg are not merely observers of life, but active participants. They take the calculated risks required to exercise leadership, and experiment with the untried. It is surprising (and most aspiring leaders do not realize it), but much failure comes from people literally standing in their own way, preventing their own progress.

Wallenberg never blocked his own path; rather, he created new paths where others saw only impenetrable walls. In the process, he was able to motivate others to do the same. He was a dispenser of hope in an environment filled with hopelessness and despair.

History is replete with instances where small, militarily weaker forces triumphed on the strength of superior strategy and tactics. Ingenuity makes surprise possible and allows quick adaptation and reaction to an adversary's actions. Without flexibility, humans are reduced to automatons, programmed only for failure.

Ingenuity requires information as its fuel. The established objective and the available tools and procedures provide the raw material for any leadership action. But much can be accomplished when leaders reach beyond traditional methods and use the status quo as a floor rather than a ceiling. Leaders must be evaluated on the basis of what they achieve. Results are what count, not formulaic adherence to precedent.

Leaders must be achievers and result-oriented. We can "do more with less" when we allow, and encourage our followers to think creatively, and not confine them to what has already been done. Military leaders are often criticized for preparing to fight the *previous* war. The best leaders think of all the possible ways in which available resources might be used or modified to achieve the objective, and expect those under them to participate, creating a group thought.

Few leaders will ever have the opportunity to help as many people as did Raoul Wallenberg. Still, each victory is immeasurably precious for those whose futures are impacted at the plants, the offices, schools, wherever our leadership shadow may fall.

They, their children, their grandchildren, their entire posterity, and all whose lives are and will be touched by you, owe their existence to that one heartbeat of time when a leader took action, despite the dangers or loss of career.

Although conditions may differ, the lessons for leadership should be valuable for all who aspire to more effective leadership. With patient application, it can be transferred and applied to everyday leadership problems, whether on the level of CEO's or individuals.

The following is an excerpt from USA Today, Thursday, March 21, 1991

WALLENBERG CASE

The Soviet Union handed Sweden, seventy hitherto secret documents on the case of missing, Swedish diplomat, Raoul Wallenberg. Wallenberg, who saved thousands of Hungarian Jews from Nazi death camps, disappeared after Soviet troops entered Budapest in the last days of World War II. Swedish radio and the documents, reportedly confirm a Soviet claim that Wallenberg died of a heart attack in a Moscow prison in 1947.

Leaders have Moral Courage

In history, we find many examples of leaders with true physical courage; but what example do we have of true moral courage? Consider the example of General Doniphan, an obscure frontier Missouri militia general, who rose from being a school teacher to a heroic figure, because of his courage to do the right things during unpopular times.

Case of Courage—The Doniphan Story

On November 1st, 1838, during the Mormon War, Missouri Militia Commander, General Lucas, ordered Mormon leaders, Joseph Smith and some followers, to be brought into the Missouri Militia's camp to be tried by a court-martial. The charges were treason. It appears rumors had spread against the religious group that they were conspiring to overthrow the government and kill Governor Boggs, the Governor of Missouri.

The charges were completely without merit, but the public opinion was against the Mormon's. Joseph Smith knew that many innocent lives would be taken if a full out war were to be conducted. He brought all the Mormon leaders together and a decision was made to pursue peace talks with the Missouri officials. Surrendering himself to the authorities, Joseph Smith was taken to stand before his accusers who were composed "of nineteen militia officers, and seventeen preachers of various sects, who had served as volunteers against the Mormons."

The trial was brief, and Joseph Smith and his associates were condemned to be shot in the public square of Far West Missouri, in the presence of their families and friends! General Doniphan, as brigadier general of the state militia, was ordered by General Lucas to execute them. General Doniphan flatly refused to carry out the orders.

General Doniphan opposed the decision of the court-martial to shoot Joseph and the other Mormon leaders. Due to his firmness and the determination that neither he, nor his brigade, should take part in "a cold-blooded murder," the lives of the Mormon leaders were spared.

General Doniphan was true to himself not only during this incident with the Mormon leader, but throughout his life. His moral courage at any time could have cost him his political career, including the financial repercussions against him. In a rare display of both physical and moral courage, General Doniphan knew the price for refusing to carry out the extermination order, could be costly. Did General Doniphan struggle with his decision? He left no records or journals behind for us to know, but I am sure he struggled; it's human. What we do know is what resulted from his actions.

I know that from my own experience as a Second Lieutenant stationed on the DMZ in Korea, I struggled with my own actions as an emerging officer.

One of my first struggles with courage came as I witnessed a rather brutal act on a member of my platoon by my Company Commander. The Captain became angry at the soldier and threw a gas mask hitting the soldier in the face, followed by verbal abuse and humiliation; while I stood by and did nothing. The soldier was helpless. He knew that if he were to retaliate, he faced severe punishment, to include possible jail time; but I could see the anger inside him fueled by the humiliation of the act. Later that night, the incident weighed heavily on my mind and I couldn't sleep.

As I was contemplating the event, I was somewhat ashamed of my inaction. I had let the fear of losing my career impact another person, but most importantly, a member of my platoon who had an element of trust in my position as his leader. I felt that his trust in me had been rightfully compromised. I was sure that not only he, but other members of the group whom I led, had lost trust in me to protect them.

During this deep period of reflection, SSG Evans, a squad leader and friend, came up to me, placed his hand on my shoulder and said, "Lieutenant, don't ever be afraid to stand up for what is right."

His words sunk deep into my conscious. For years afterwards, I worried because I didn't have the courage to stand up to the Captain, but I resolved to never lose courage again when it came to principle and people.

Years later while stationed in Panama, I faced another incident which would test my courage, as a Captain in command of a joint task force. My mission was to escort three, U.S. Army Landing Craft (LCM), up the Gulf of Darien, to a forward operations base commanded by the Panamanians in the remote jungle town of El Real, between Panama and Columbia. We were to provide ammunition and medical supplies to the Panamanian Defense Force (PDF) conducting drug raids against the Columbian Cartels. General Manuel Noriega, then dictator of Panama, had appointed one of his officers to accompany our task force. His name was **Major Giroldi. Our boat LCM commander was a bright and lively U.S. Army Transportation Lieutenant. As the task force commander, I was responsible for the group and getting the supplies to the joint task force at El Real. The first part of the trip was uneventful.

We departed the Panama Canal Zone into the Pacific Ocean, following the coastline to the Gulf of Darien. The PDF Major spent most of his time sleeping on our upper deck near the wheel house. As we approached the estuary for the final trip up the swollen muddy river to El Real, the Major became alive and began to take command; he cursed and intimidated the soldiers on the boat. He berated them, focusing on the young Lieutenant harder than the others, claiming they were soft and could never serve under a Panamanian Officer.

After about ten minutes, I had heard enough. I stepped over and stood nose to nose with the Major and demanded that he stop his tirades, that it was not necessary, and if he had problems to direct them to me.

For a while it seemed to calm him down. As we approached the base, he must have felt a strong need to, once more, show his power and authority. In a near frenzy-like action, he started throwing ropes at the soldiers, barking commands, cursing. Then he grabbed the Lieutenant by the shirt and started to walk to the front of the open ramp. Instinctively, I stepped in front of the Major.

While his crew looked on, I pulled the Lieutenant away from his hold, ordered the boat to stop and said, "Major Giroldi, I don't know what you are doing but as long as I am here, you will never touch or yell at these men again. I am turning these boats around right now—you can come with us or I will drop you off at the shore, which will it be?" There was a blistering moment of silence; his brown eyes pierced my soul. "What is it to be," I demanded. Nothing—just his dead glare at me.

"Lieutenant, take the boat to El Real, we are going to drop the Major off and return down river."

We dropped Major Giroldi and his group off at El Real and returned down river. My final view of the Major was of him waving his hands, walking towards the operations center. A short distance down the river and around the bend, I had the boats drop anchor and radioed our situation to the 193rd Infantry Brigade Tactical Operations Center, located at Ft. Clayton, Panama.

There were minor consequences to my actions due to the political nature of our operation, but I also had a great deal of support. It had been a risky decision, but the right one in my mind. It was a decision that tested a personal commitment I had made to myself years before. I had made a promise never to allow my fears and self-interest to hurt others. I was a leader, who had impact on others. If they could not trust me to protect them, who could they trust?

"Leaders do not react to fear, they act on the principles of right and wrong."

We fulfilled our mission and I returned to El Real that night. I never saw Major Giroldi again, but the lesson was driven home. Leadership requires courage and risk; the hardest being moral courage. Since that incident, I have never experienced failed courage in defending others. The truth is that once you have stepped up, it is easy afterwards. Having courage feels good. I learned this one principle:

> **Doing nothing wrong is not the same as doing the right thing**

The reality with courage is that it becomes easier as we learn to drive our fears out and our convictions in. Decisions become better and those around us respect who we are.

Later I would have similar experiences while assigned to the Chilean War Academy in Santiago Chile. I arrived at the end of the Pinochet reign and met Mario Morales and other academy staff officers who had served under his regime.

At the time the world was criticizing the Pinochet coup that started on September 11, 1973 with the overthrow of Salvador Allende. Most of these officers had been lieutenants at the time and were involved with rounding up suspected subversives and taking them to the National Stadium in Santiago, which had been turned by the military into an ad hoc prison camp, where prisoners were interrogated, tortured, tried and executed. Two American detainees were the AP reporter Charles Horman and Frank Teruggi who is believed to have been victims of the regimes' purges and whose bodies have never been recovered.

The officers shared with me that their orders were to round up over 30,000 Chilean citizen suspects and take them to the National Stadium for interrogation and trial. These junior officers were responsible for overseeing the operation at the street level and as result 3000 Chilean citizens were eventually killed and another 1000 unaccounted for. Some of the officers justified the actions as necessary for national security or patriotic obligation while others like Mario felt a dark sense of shame and remorse. He would tell me later that the remorse was caused by is inaction, his failure to act against orders he would come to know were wrong and immoral.

The stories of failed courage and the atrocities committed in the name of national security made me realize how leadership at the top influences the actions of followers down the chain. While it is easy to use this as an excuse, the truth is that we are individually accountable for our actions. There had been good moral Chilean officers who were removed, retired and in some cases executed for their failure to participate, choosing to exercise rarely seen personal courage that cost them everything. Mario's' guilt may have been result of those who chose to stand up and against actions that were morally wrong.

Courage and Character

While stationed in Panama, I had the chance to work with U.S. Rep. Ike Skelton (D-MO), from Missouri. Representative Skelton was in Panama to gather facts concerning the role and future of the famous School of Americas, which at that time was located in Panama. It was a school designed to train foreign officers from around Central and South America in counter-insurgency, irregular warfare, psychological-operations, and combat arms orientation.

On one of our trips together, I had the opportunity to ask him a few questions that had been on my mind. I asked him what he felt was the most important thing he did as a United States Representative?

Without hesitation the answer came, "Taking care of people", I then asked another question. "What is the most important characteristic a leader needs as a Senator, Congressman, or an Army Officer?"

"Courage".

Having the courage to take care of the individual is not always popular or easy as a politician, especially when special interest groups launch artful media attacks against you, when they don't get their way, or where opponents are always looking for cracks in your armor.

Senator Skelton shared with me several incidents from his life that also had impact on him and helped to define his courage; specifically as a member of the Armed Services Committee, issues and situations he faced that challenged his moral courage.

At the end of our discussion, he made the comment, "Captain Shelton, more than any time in our military history, we need men and women of character and courage," and then with a pause, he declared, "We need men and women who understand sacrifice, I am afraid that money and things have robbed us of that."

Over the years, I have learned to respond to the whisperings of my conscience. I have lived my life in such a way, that I can listen to those internal promptings and have the courage to do as it instructs. Of course I have continued to face fear, experience ridicule, and meet opposition. The difference is that I have the courage to defy the consensus; the courage to stand for principle.

A moral coward is one who is afraid to do what he thinks is right, because others will disapprove or laugh. Remember, all men have their fears, but those who face their fears with dignity have courage.

As leaders, you are regularly required to make choices on the basis of what you know to be right. We are free in most instances, to make our own decisions, but we are never free to determine the final outcomes of our choices.

It is not enough for us to know what is right and to believe it is good. We must be willing to stand up and be counted. We must be willing to act in accordance with what we believe under all circumstances. It is of little value for us to believe one way if we behave contrary to that belief in our private actions, or in our business performance. Today, it requires great courage to be an effective leader. For many it is not easy, and it will likely not become easier. The tests of our day are severe. This is particularly so for young, emerging leaders.

Being true to correct leadership principles does not always make us popular, but I can almost guarantee it will be admired. Having the courage of our convictions has its own rewards. It brings satisfaction and fulfillment into our lives, rather than discouragement and defeat. As a leader you do not want to ever have the heavy weight of regret on your shoulders.

Note: **

During Operation Just Cause—On October 3, 1989. A coup attempt against General Manuel Noriega instigated by Major Giroldi failed. Maj. Giroldi was summarily executed by General Noriega after the General failed to convince the Major to commit suicide.

Chapter 11

Being Offended

Choose Not to Be Offended

I have seen good leaders become poor decision makers as result of being offended. As leaders, when we believe or say we have been offended, we usually mean we feel insulted, mistreated, snubbed, or disrespected. Certainly clumsy, embarrassing, unprincipled, and mean-spirited things do occur in our interactions with other people at work, at home and at social gatherings, which would allow us to take offense. However, as leaders you cannot allow those above you or who work for you, to offend you. We make the choice to be offended, thus submitting ourselves to poor decision making, and leaving ourselves open to poor judgment. Nothing clouds a leader's decision making more than allowing understand this one principle: **Being Offended is a choice**.

As leaders, we have moral agency . . . the capacity for independent action and choice. Our ability to make choices requires leaders to act, and not just be acted upon. As a leader, to believe that our superior or a follower can *make* us feel offended, angry, hurt, or bitter, diminishes our ability to control our decision making, and transforms us into ineffective leaders to be acted upon. As leaders, you have the power to act and to choose how you will respond to an offense.

> "To be offended is a choice we make; it is not a condition inflicted or imposed upon us by someone or something else."
>
> **Dr. David Allen Bednar**

On many occasions during the civil war, President Lincoln elected not to be offended. In one example during the early years of the civil war:

Avoid Being Offended

> Lincoln went to the residence of General Grant to discuss the poor performance of his army. Lincoln waited several hours for the general to arrive home.
>
> When Grant arrived, he was informed that the President was waiting. For unknown reasons, Grant chose to ignore the President, going directly to his bedroom without visiting with Lincoln retiring for the night.
>
> When finally informed that Grant had retired to bed, the President responded by suggesting, "The General had a lot on his mind, and probably needed the rest."

Lincoln did not let the offense act on him; he maintained control of the otherwise tense situation. Lincoln mastered the principle of not becoming offended. This characteristic may very well have been the key to his ability to make good decisions.

An example is that of Benedict Arnold, who was a personal favorite and friend of George Washington. Arnold, who had been a successful field commander under Washington, was brilliant in the field; however his pride and inability to handle offenses caused him to lose everything. Arnold's downfall began as a number of junior officers received promotions to Brigadier General above him, leaving him behind. He became offended. Arnold would go on to win major battles against the British and was promoted with his seniority restored; but he was already too angry to forgive Congress, and never would.

Benedict Arnolds Betrayal

By May of 1779, Arnold made contact with the British to hand over the defense plans of West Point. Why would a man commit treason against his country, especially one who had fought so valiantly?

He was offended, angry, and hurt over the many slights he received over the years. He felt unappreciated by his country and those he fought with, even sacrificing his own leg for the cause. His pride was most likely the biggest part of his life that was damaged—humiliation was always an affront Arnold could never take. Money, of course, played a big part. He was offered in excess of 10,000 pounds and a commission in the British military.

The British provided handsomely for Arnold, but never completely trusted him. He was never given an important military command. He and his wife moved to London, where he found no job, some admiration, and some contempt.

He eventually moved his family to Canada, where he reentered the shipping business. The Tories there disliked him and had no use for him, and eventually he returned his family to London. When the fighting began between France and England, he tried again for military service, but to no avail.

His shipping ventures eventually failed and he died in 1801, virtually unknown, his wife joining him in death three years later.

Arnold allowed himself to be acted upon, and the eventual results were betrayal to his country and misery. Compare to Abraham Lincoln, who was a leader who exercised his agency and acted in accordance with effective leadership principles of not being offended; Lincoln became a mighty instrument in American history.

The capacity to conquer offense may seem beyond most leaders reach. This capability, however, is not reserved for, or restricted to, prominent leaders; it can and should be exercised at every level of leadership down even to the front-line supervisor and manager.

Perfecting our ability to avoid the pitfalls of being offended, I would suggest that we will spend our entire life learning how to lead without being offended. Every position we attain is a learning laboratory, and a workshop in which we gain experience as we practice the ongoing process of perfecting our leadership.

An inexperienced leader learns valuable lessons as he leads both supportive as well as non-supportive followers, and thereby becomes a more effective leader. A new or young leader learns how to be a leader through experience, and by working with other leaders and followers who wholeheartedly support him, even while recognizing his inexperience.

Understanding that the workplace is a learning laboratory helps us to prepare for an inevitable reality. In some way and at some time, someone in the workplace will do or say something that could be considered offensive. Such an event will surely happen to each and every one of us—and it certainly will occur more than once. Much of how we are respected and viewed as leaders will depend on how we react to those offenses.

You and I cannot control the intentions or behavior of other people. However, we do determine how we will act. Remember that as leaders, you and I are free to make choices and we can choose not to be offended. An option that is not acceptable is for a leader to get even.

> **"If you are going to kill a man, dig two graves, one for you and one for the other"**
>
> *Chinese Proverb—Author Unknown*

Example from the First Iraq War

A more current example of this leadership principle was seen during the first Iraq war.

Gulf War General Schwarzkopf vs. Colon Powell

At the start of the Gulf Was an exchange of words and communications occurred between General Norman Schwarzkopf, and Colon Powell, the Secretary of Defense.

General Schwarzkopf, whose army was suffering because of inadequate logistical support, had a sharp exchange of words with Powell, by the way of condemnation and criticism that accused Powell of thoughtlessness, slothfulness, and neglect.

Powell might easily have resented Schwarzkopf and his message, but he chose not to take offense. Powell responded compassionately, and described how Congress was divided in how to deploy the troops and equipment of which Schwarzkopf was not aware.

Powell responded, "I know you are under a lot of pressure and it bothers me that we can't act quicker, you're criticism is understood. I am not mad, but am glad to have a general of your caliber heading the Army."

One of the greatest indicators of our own leadership maturity is revealed in how we respond to the weaknesses, the inexperience, and the potentially offensive actions of others. A thing, an event, or an expression may be offensive, but you and I can choose not to be offended, and to say with General Powell, "I am not mad or angry."

Clearly, the rigorous requirements that lead to effective leadership for you, includes experiences that test and challenge us. If a follower says or does something that we consider offensive, our first obligation is to refuse to take offense and then communicate privately, honestly, and directly with that individual. Such an approach builds trust, respect, and permits misperceptions to be clarified leaving true intent to be understood.

In today's fast-paced business world, there seems to be a greater tendency for people to act aggressively toward each other. Some are quick to take offense, and respond angrily to real or imagined affronts, and we've all experienced or heard reports of managers who fly into rages, or other examples of rude, insensitive behavior, that undermine a leader's respect and trust with followers.

Leaders who struggle with unbalanced aggressiveness can learn a lesson from Viktor Frank. Reflecting on his horrendous, wartime experiences, Viktor Frank recalled:

> **"We, who lived in concentration camps, can remember the men who walked through the huts comforting others, giving away their last piece of bread."**

They may have been few in number, but they offer sufficient proof that everything can be taken from a man but one thing: the last of the human freedoms—*to choose one's attitude in any given set of circumstances, is to choose one's own way."*

Case of Reacting vs. Acting

> **While serving as the Director of Human Resources for a large company, I had an experience that taught me a great leadership lesson regarding being offended as a front-line leader.**
>
> **I was preparing a disciplinary action against a supervisor who had been with the organization for over ten years. The supervisor had been charged with verbally abusing one of his workers, and was facing termination because of his actions.**

While investigating the incident, I asked what led him to use fowl and abusive language. He shared his story with me. While starting daily operations, one of his more vocal employees made a sarcastic and disrespectful remark to a fellow worker regarding the supervisor. It was equally as vulgar, and the supervisor had heard the comments.

When he approached the employee regarding the remarks, the employee became disrespectful again, intensifying the supervisors anger. The supervisor asked himself, what have I done to deserve this?

Unfortunately, the supervisor reacted with a verbal string of language that was personal and racial. As I listened to the supervisor, I remembered the leadership principle on the importance of acting instead of reacting, to the events around us. The supervisor had made a fundamental mistake by reacting. I asked him why he did not pull the employee aside and act. I told him that an appropriate action was to ask the employee, "Help me understand why you made the comments that you did"? He had no answer.

The problem was he failed to act rather than react.

That experience demonstrated for me that in most encounters, leaders can determine the kind of experience they are going to have by how they respond. It was tragic that this supervisor reacted the way he did, it not only cost him his job, but the negative impact to the organization in lost talent and loss of trust for management was costly.

As front-line leaders who have power and authority, it is in the workplace that our behavior is most significant. It is the place where our actions have the greatest impact. Sometimes we are so filled with power, pride, or ego that we no longer guard our words or our actions. We forget simple civility. If we are not on guard, we can fall into the habit of criticizing, losing our tempers, or behaving selfishly.

When leaders become offended and demonstrate that offense through power and abuse, employees may be quick to forgive because they work for them, have an implied obligation, or because of job security; but they often carry away, in silence, unseen injuries and unspoken resentment towards the leader.

There are too many workplaces where workers fear their leaders because of their reactions to perceived offenses. This fear leads to the fostering of a work environment and atmosphere of contention, conflict, and contempt in the workplace. It diminishes any trust or respect that workers may have for those leaders.

Leaders must set the example of maintaining emotional control in every setting, and not let offense control their actions. In the face of criticism and implications, the leader must maintain his composure, refusing to act unkindly or disrespectfully.

Many leaders, who most need to hear this message about choosing not to be offended, are probably not reading this or any other, like literature. We all have met them, and have seen the effects of leaders who have been offended and the actions that followed. If you have a problem with this principle, work hard to control it and be not offended.

Chapter 12

Mid-Eastern Leadership

The Western perception of Islamic leadership or Middle Eastern leadership is often misunderstood and in some circles associated with the support of violence and terrorism, masking the truth, that Islamic leadership is based on a religion of peace. Mid-Eastern or Islamic leadership has a very comprehensive set of values and concepts that are centered on faith and values according to God.

Causes of this misunderstanding may be caused by the fact that the West been has been successful in providing leadership literature to the world while there is very little literature available regarding our Eastern friends in terms of the preferred leadership experience.

Comparing the literature that is available suggest that there is no difference in individual preferred leadership style between the east and west, the motivators are the same, the impact of styles is similar and what is effective in the west is equally effective in the east, so what is the difference? It's all about how culture impacts groups.

The significance of culture on a society is that, like an individual, culture is a more or less consistent pattern of thought and action. Within each culture there come into being characteristic purposes not necessarily shared by other types of society. In obedience to their purposes, each people further and further consolidates its experience, and in proportion to the urgency of these drives the heterogeneous items of behavior take more and more congruous shape. However, culture can be usurped by individual experiences and beliefs when those experiences are personal. That is why in the most hostile cultures with low tolerance a kind act to an individual can have more weight than the collective cultural beliefs and that is why preferred leadership techniques and styles have universal appeal.

It is important to understand and analyze the Arab world from its cultural aspects regarding social trends and expectations that demonstrates why the Muslim faith plays a significant role in the people's lives more so than it does in the Christian West. This is not to say that the Christian faith is or does not have an importance in people's lives, the difference is Christianity is confined to and viewed as having its place in the home not to be intrusive outside, while the Muslim faith is expected to be in the home nor does it set boundaries outside the home and family to include public and institutional application. There are two dynamics that define Islamic culture; religion and social structure.

Religion

Islam is a Muslim's Way of Life. They (Muslims) foster Islamic ideals and values in everything they do. It is both religion and a code of life that is adherent to Gods commands without objections. Islam literally means "Peace through Submission to God" it is absolute truth. A Muslim believes in all the recognized prophets of both the Jews and Christians as well as all revelations, with Prophet Mohammad (PBUH) as the last prophet who completed the last of Gods message to humanity through the Qur'an. The two sources of principles and practices that make up Islam are the Qur'an and Mohammad's (PBUH) example as written in the Hadith a record compiled by those who were directly with him that also constitutes the Shari'ah (Islamic Law from Qur'an and Traditions). This law is the ultimate truth and includes guiding principles in ways of worship, family, dress, finance and social relationships.

At the core Muslims embrace practices called the five pillars of Islam—the testimony, offering prayers, paying Zakat (alms-giving to the poor), performing Hajj (pilgrimage to Makkah) and Sawm (Fasting). It is this religious view that provides the basics for leadership that has its core purpose as Service for Humanity. Islam suggests that a Leader does not seek for his own interest but for the best welfare of others.

He does not serve for himself but for what God wills him to do so. It is only God that tells leaders the purpose and mission in this world. Because Islam is presented as the ultimate truth, its impact is deeply woven into the social fabric at all levels.

Social Structure

The Arab social structure is power centered in that the less powerful members of organizations and institutions (like the family) accept and expect that power is distributed unequally partly due to the fact that it is simply Gods will to have order and direction and that followers have been pre-ordained to leadership, status and life situations. As result this causes unplanned inequality amongst the group and suggests that a society's level of inequality is endorsed by the followers as much as by the leaders. Power and inequality are extremely fundamental facts of any society and anybody with some international experience will be aware that 'all societies are unequal, but some are more unequal than others'.

Arab social structure is more likely to follow a caste system that does not allow significant upward mobility of its citizens. They are also highly rule-oriented with laws, rules, regulations, and controls in order to reduce the amount of uncertainty, while inequalities of power and wealth have been allowed to grow within the society.

Unlike religious views and teachings, when the two dimensions of power and wealth are combined, it creates a situation where leaders have virtually ultimate power and authority, and the rules, laws and regulations developed by those in power reinforce their own leadership and control. It is not unusual for new leadership to arise from insurrection—the ultimate power, rather than from diplomatic or democratic change as witnessed in the 2011-2012 Arabic Spring that affected Egypt, Libya and Syria.

There tends to be a high level of inequality of power and wealth within the society which is determined by **Power—Distance** concerns. The distance between then elite and the people base determines equity and fairness. These populations have an expectation and acceptance that leaders will separate themselves from the group and this condition is not necessarily subverted upon the population, but rather accepted by the society as their cultural heritage. The Arab Spring was a result of Power Distance where rebellion and insurrection resulted.

Arab social structure is also defined by its social tolerance for uncertainty and ambiguity; it ultimately refers to man's search for Truth. It indicates to what extent a culture programs its members to feel either uncomfortable or comfortable in unstructured situations. Unstructured situations are novel, unknown, surprising, and different from usual. This sense of uncertainty avoiding cultures try to minimize the possibility of such situations by strict laws and rules, safety and security measures, and on the philosophical and religious level by a belief in absolute Truth; 'there can only be one Truth and we have it', this phenomena can also be found in certain social groups in America, such as Fundamentalists etc. but is less predominant in the whole American social structure. Citizens in Arabic countries are also more emotional, and motivated by inner nervous energy. The opposite type, uncertainty accepting cultures, such as Europe are more tolerant of opinions different from what they are used to; they try to have as few rules as possible, and on the philosophical and religious level they are relativist and allow many currents to flow side by side. People within these cultures are more phlegmatic and contemplative, and not expected by their environment to express emotions.

Arabic culture emphasizes the society's low level of tolerance for uncertainty. In an effort to minimize or reduce this level of uncertainty, strict rules, laws, policies, and regulations are adopted and implemented. The ultimate goal of these populations is to control everything in order to eliminate or avoid the unexpected. As a result of this high Uncertainty Avoidance characteristic, the society does not readily accept change and is very risk adverse.

In contrast to the power centeredness of the Arab World is the low ranking for Individualism, which translates into a collectivist society as compared to Individualist culture and is manifested in a close long-term commitment to the member 'group', that being a family, extended family, or extended relationships. Loyalty in a collectivist culture is paramount, and over-rides most other societal rules.

Individualism on the one side versus its opposite, collectivism, that is the degree to which individuals are integrated into groups. On the individualist side we find societies such as Europe and the United

States (west), in which the ties between individuals are loose: everyone is expected to look after him/herself and his/her immediate family. Christians and in particular Protestant Christians from their incepting have taught that their salvation is their responsibility as individuals and not the collective group, making the point that no one outside the individual has the right to interfere or make corrections to individual choices.

On the collectivist side, found predominately in Arabic cultures, we find societies in which people from birth onwards are integrated into strong, cohesive in-groups, often extended families (with uncles, aunts and grandparents) which continue protecting them in exchange for unquestioning loyalty. The word 'collectivism' in this sense has no political meaning: it refers to the group, not to the state. Again, the issue addressed by this dimension is an extremely fundamental one, regarding all societies in the world.

A major cultural distinction in the East is the cultural focus on masculinity versus its opposite, femininity, referring to the distribution of roles between the genders which is another fundamental issue for any society to which a range of solutions are found. Studies revealed that women's values differ less among societies than men's values; men's values from one country to another contain a dimension from very assertive and competitive and maximally different from women's values on the one side, to modest and caring and similar to women's values on the other. The assertive pole has been called 'masculine' and the modest, caring pole 'feminine'.

The women in feminine countries have the same modest, caring values as the men; in the masculine countries they are somewhat assertive and competitive, but not as much as the men, so that these countries show a gap between men's values and women's values. In the Arabic culture the masculinity value is predominate opposed to what we find in the West. This would indicate that while women in the Arab World are limited in their rights, it may be due more to cultural paradigm rather than the Muslim religion.

Impact on Leadership

As result of the power distance, uncertainty avoidance and feminine avoidance, Mid-East surveys show that leaders do well in training, development, governance, and structure but are challenged in supervision, communication, conflict resolution, empowerment and engagement in the workforce.

The employees under these leadership paradigms tend to respect the position and the person sitting in the supervisor's seat is caring and well-meaning, a large majority feel that their superiors are not role models, do not stand up for what they believe in, and do not support and help the development of their people as they should. This dimension, along with accountability tends to be weak.

Another culturally created barrier for leadership is accountability; surveys show that mid-eastern leadership tends not to place heavy emphasis on accountability, nor helps people live up to it and do not create systems to allow accountability to function, rather preference is placed on relationship building, avoiding confrontation and accusation. There tends to be little value placed on employee feedback, 360 engagements, communication forums, personal coaching or meaningful development of the people. Workers tend to find less satisfaction and feel less ownership, partly due to the above mentioned lack of accountability and authority to impact business outcomes contributed to the power distance creating excessive internal friction, rules, duplication, regulations and bureaucracy.

The impact is on the front line leaders who do not receive regular feedback and guidance on their work, and open communication channels to review and clarify management intent before acting with their group which causes a perception of non-engagement with employees sufficiently to clarify and seek input on the direction they are giving causing lack of transparency and employee participation.

Culture Impacts Tolerance

Given the role culture plays in forming opinions and social actions does not necessarily define how people will behave in terms of moral actions. Leadership consists of moral actions that have cause and effect actions with individuals. While the culture can define how people dress, act and react, it does not have total control of how people define their core beliefs as individuals.

Given the cultural differences do not impact core principles of effective leadership and it cross cultural impact? There are certain behaviors that cross all cultural barriers such as kindness, gratitude, giving, concern for others, individual consideration, constructive communications, all these and many more have proven to be effective in all cultures through history and current society's. Let me share with you some examples through Islamic Leaders who have had a positive impact on mankind.

An effective leader who is recognized by the Suni, led with compassion and consideration for the people was Umar ibn al-Khattāb or Umar of Saudi Arabia who was the friend of the Islamic prophet, Muhammad. Umar became the successor of the Islamic nations after Muhammad's death. His leadership effectiveness is without question one of the true pillars of effectiveness in its style and application. Born of middle class status but despite literacy being uncommon in pre-Islamic Arabia, Umar learned to read and write in his youth. Though not a poet himself, he developed a love for poetry and literature. Umar learned martial arts, horse riding and wrestling. He was tall and physically powerful and was soon to become a renowned wrestler. He became a merchant and made several journeys to Rome and Persia, where he studied and observed various scholars and analyzed the Roman and Persian societies closely.

Around 610 AD, ISLAM had not been fully accepted by the popular leaders of the time. Umar went to those who opposed Islam near Mecca and explained the positive qualities of Islam and its benefit to social order and acceptance of one God. Showing great courage of conviction, Umar thereafter openly prayed as the chiefs, reportedly watched in anger. This further helped the Muslims to gain confidence in practicing Islam openly. With disregard for his own safety, Umar challenged anyone who dared to stop the Muslims from praying, although no one dared to interfere with Umar when he was openly praying.

Umar's conviction in helping others and his devotion to Islam proved to be an example for others and gave power to the Muslims and the faith in Mecca. It was after this that Muslims offered prayers openly for the first time. A future leader of the Muslims, Abdullah bin Masoud said;

> Umar's embracing Islam was our victory, his migration to Medina was our success and his reign a blessing from Allah, we didn't offer prayers in Al-Haram Mosque until Umar accepted Islam, when he accepted Islam Quraish were compelled to let us pray in the Mosque.
>
> *Abdullah Bin Masoud*

In 624 Umar participated in the first Battle between Muslims and Quraish

Umar was a citizen warrior in the defense of what he believed and participated in the battle with the local Quraishi army. Later in the year Umar was a part of campaign against the Jewish tribe of Banu Nadir. In 627 he participated in the Battle of the Trench and also in the Battle of Banu Qurayza. His devotion to his people became known throughout the land and became an example of dedication and service.

Umar's political genius first manifested as the architect of keeping the Muslim nation together after the death of Muhammad by unifying the different factions threatening to destroy the Muslim movement.

He became a popular figure with the everyday Muslim but was not a very popular figure among the notables of Madinah and members of Majlis al Shura, accordingly succession of Umar was initially discouraged by high ranking officials and he soon found himself openly defying the establishments of non-Muslims Nevertheless, Umar, was well known for his extraordinary will power, intelligence, political astuteness, impartiality, justice and care for poor and underprivileged people.

The famous Muslim leader Abu Bakr is reported to have said to the high-ranking advisers:

> His (Umar's) strictness was there because of my softness when the weight of Caliphate will be over his shoulders he will remain no longer strict. If I will be asked by the God to whom I have appointed my successor, I will tell him that I have appointed the best man among your men.
>
> *Abu Bakr*

Umar became the accepted leader of Islam and was thus not as troublesome as any of the others. His was perhaps one of the smoothest transitions to power from one authority to another in the Muslim lands.

Upon becoming the leader of Islam, Umar addressed the Muslims in his Inaugural address as:

> The mantle of Leadership has fallen on my shoulders. I swear it before God that I never coveted this office. I wished that it would have devolved on some other person more worthy than me. But now that in national interest, the responsibility for leading the Muslims has come to vest in me, I assure you that I will not run away from my post, and will make an earnest effort to discharge the onerous duties of the office to the best of my capacity in accordance with the injunctions of Islam.
>
> God has examined me from you and you from me, in the performance of my duties; I will seek guidance from the Scriptures, and will follow the examples set by the Holy Prophets. In this task I seek your assistance. If I follow the right path, follow me. If I deviate from the right path, correct me so that we are not led astray.

Umar understood accountability and integrity. Umar was a gifted orator, and he would use his ability to get a soft corner in the hearts of people. Umar was amerced in the people, he often led prayers and gave uplifting talks, and one of his most memorable was when he addresses the poor gathered around him:

Umar's Leadership Addressing the Poor

Brethren, it has come to my notice that the people are afraid of me . . . . They say that he (Umar) has become the Leader now; God knows how hard he will be.

Whoever has said this is not wrong in his assessment . . . . know ye brethren that you will feel a change in me. For those who practice tyranny and deprive others of their rights, I will be harsh and stern, but for those who follow the law, I will be most soft and tender.

I will be harsh and stern against the aggressor but I will be a pillar of strength for the weak. I will not calm down until I will put one cheek of a tyrant on the ground and the other under my feet, and for the poor and weak, I will put my cheek on the ground.

Umar ibn al-Khattāb

Umar's focus was on the well-being of poor and underprivileged people, as this class made a bulk of the community, the people were soundly moved by Umar's concern and his speeches so that his popularity grew rapidly and continuously over the period of his reign. In addition to this Umar, in order to establish equality and fairness to all declared that the thousands of prisoners from rebel and apostate tribes who had been taken away as slaves during previous conflicts and wars were to be freed and ordered general amnesty for the prisoners, and their immediate emancipation.

On another occasion during an open address to the people he demonstrated his great commitment to all people and to their need for justice and democracy:

> He that is weakest among you shall be in my eye the strongest, until I have vindicated for him his rights; he that is strongest I will treat as the weakest, until he complies with the law.
>
> *Umar ibn al-Khattāb*

Umar's challenge was to bring the military under control and as the Commander-in-chief of the army he addressed them collectively saying:

> Remember, I have not appointed you as commanders and tyrants over the people. I have sent you as leaders instead, so that the people may follow your example. Give the Muslims their rights and do not beat them lest they become abused.
>
> Do not praise them unduly, lest they fall into the error of conceit. Do not keep your doors shut in their faces, lest the more powerful of them eat up the weaker ones. And do not behave as if you were superior to them, for that is tyranny over them.
>
> *Umar ibn al-Khattāb*

Various other strict codes of conducts were to be obeyed by the governors and state officials. The principal officers were required to come to Mecca during Hajj, during which people were free to present any complaint against them. In order to minimize the chances of corruption, Umar made it a point to pay high salaries to the staff.

While under his leadership, the empire was expanding at an unprecedented rate, he also began to build the political structure that would hold together the vast empire that was being built. He undertook many administrative reforms and closely oversaw public policy. He established an advanced administration for the newly conquered lands, including several new ministries and bureaucracies, and ordered a census of all the Muslim territories.

Other notable acts of compassion included the relocation of certain Christian and Jewish communities of Najran and Khaybar following a decade of slaughter, allowing them to reside in Syria or Iraq. He issued orders that these Christians and Jews should be treated well and allotted them the equivalent land in their new settlements. In 641, he established financial institution and started annual allowance for the Muslims.

A year later he also started allowance for the poor, underprivileged and old non-Muslim citizens of the empire. As a leader, 'Umar was known for his simple, austere lifestyle. Rather than adopt the pomp and display affected by the rulers of the time, he continued to live much as he had when Muslims were poor and persecuted.

His compassion and concern for his followers was demonstrated again in 638, Arabia fell into severe drought followed by a famine. The population around the country side began to die because of hunger and epidemic disease. Hundreds of thousands of people from all over Arabia gathered at Madinah where food was rationed. Soon the reserves of food at Madinah began to decline, and Umar wrote to the provincial governors of Syria, Palestine and Iraq for aid. A state of emergency was declared in Madinah and Arabia. The timely aid of Umar's governors saved the lives of thousands of people throughout Arabia. The first governor to respond was Abu Ubaidah ibn al-Jarrah, the governor of Syria. He sent a historic letter to Umar saying:

> **"I am sending you the Caravans whose one end will be here at Syria and the other will be at Madina."**
>
> *Ubaidah*

Ubaidah paid a personal visit to Medina and acted as an officer of which was headed personally by Umar. Once an adequate supply of rations reached Medina, Umar dispatched his men to the routes of Iraq, Palestine and Syria to take the supply caravans to the desert settlements deeper into Arabia, which in turn saved millions from starvation. For internally displaced people, Umar hosted a dinner every night at Medina, which according to one estimate had attendance of more than hundred thousand people.

By early 639 conditions begun to improve, Arabia received precipitation and as soon as the famine ended, Umar personally supervised the rehabilitation of the displaced people. They were given adequate amounts of rations and were exempted from payment of taxes for that year and the next year.

Tragically in 644, Umar was assassinated by Persians. His last words before he died were recorded:

Umar's Last Words

Be kind and generous to the people. Those out of them, who are good, be good to them; those who are bad overlook their lapses. Be good to the people of the conquered lands. They are the outer line of our defense; they are the target of the anger and distress of our enemies. They contribute to our revenues. They should be taxed only on their surplus wealth.

Be gracious to the Bedouins (native nomads) as they are the backbone of the Arab nation. I instruct you to be good to the Jews for they are your responsibility. Do not tax them beyond their capacity. Fear God, and in all that you do keep His will in view. In the matter of people fear God, and in the matters of God do not be afraid of the people.

With regard to the people, I enjoin upon you to administer justice with an even hand. See that all the legitimate requirements of the people are met. Be concerned for their welfare. Ensure the safety of their person and property. See that the frontiers of our domains are not violated. Take strong steps to guard the frontiers. In the matter of administration do not prefer the rich to the poor. Be hard against those who violate the law. Show them no mercy. Do not rest content until you have brought the miscreants to book.

Treat all the people as equal. Be a pillar of strength for those who are weak and oppressed. Those who are strong but do wrong, make them pay for their wrong-doings. In the distribution of wealth and other matters be above nepotism. Let no consideration of relationship or selfish interest weigh with you. Satan is at large; he may tempt you. Rise above all temptations and perform your duties in accordance with the injunctions of Islam.

Get guidance from the Scriptures. Freely consult the wise men around you. Apply your own mind in difficult cases, and seek light from God. Be simple in your living and your habits. Let there be no show or ostentation about you. Lead life as a model Muslim. As you are the leader of the Muslims, justify your leadership by being the best among them all. May God bless you.

As a leader, 'Umar was known for his simple, austere lifestyle. Rather than adopt the pomp and display affected by the rulers of the time, he continued to live much as he had when Muslims were poor and persecuted. 'Umar was vigorous, robust and a very tall man, in markets he would tower above the people.

One of Umars lasting legacys was his humility compared to Abraham Lincoln. During the siege of Jerusalem, Umar was asked to take control of the city from the Byzantine Patriarch of Jerusalem Sophronius.

Umar Legacy of Leadership

Umar went to Jerusalem with his slave. They were having one camel on which each of them rode by turn.

When Umar was entering Jerusalem it happened to be the slave's turn to ride on the camel. Though the slave offered his turn to Umar he refused and remarked: "The honor of Islam (i.e., being Muslim) is enough for all of us."

He entered Jerusalem holding the rope of the camel on which was riding his slave. His clothes were dirty and there were several patches on them.

Social Responsibility and Accountability

Umar's view of his responsibilities moved him to speak out against social injustices as well as the social impact on the less influential. He monitored public policy and kept the needs of the public central to his leadership approach. As the leader of Islam, he refused to chop off the hands of the thieves because he felt he had fallen short of his responsibility to provide meaningful employment to all his subjects. As a ruler of a vast kingdom, His vision was to ensure that every one in his kingdom should sleep on a full stomach.

> **If a dog dies hungry on the banks of the River Euphrates, Umar will be responsible for dereliction of duty.**
> *Umar*

He also knew that just having a vision is not enough unless it is supported by effective strategies. He didn't only have a vision; he truly transformed his vision into actions. For example, to ensure that nobody sleeps hungry in his empire, he used to walk through the streets almost every night to see if there is any one needy or ill."

Omar proved to be a leader of great powers of mind, inflexible integrity, and fair justice. In the simplicity of his habits, and his contempt for all pomp and luxury, he emulated the example of a concerned leader. He endeavored incessantly to impress the merit and policy of the same in his letters to his generals. 'Beware,' he would say, 'of Persian luxury, both in food and raiment. Keep to the simple habits of your country, and God will continue you victorious; depart from them, and he will reverse your fortunes.' It was his strong conviction of the truth of this policy which made him so severe in punishing all ostentatious style and luxurious indulgence in his officers.

Some of his ordinances do credit to his heart as well as his head. He forbade that any female captive who had borne a child should be sold as a slave. In his weekly distributions of the surplus money of his treasury he proportioned them to the wants, not the merits of the applicants. 'God,' said he, 'has bestowed the good things of this world to relieve our necessities, not to reward our virtues: those will be rewarded in another world.

In daily life he refused the rewards of the good, his food consisted of barley-bread or dates; his drink was water; he preached in a gown that was torn or tattered in twelve places; and a Persian satrap, who paid his homage as to the conqueror, found him asleep among the beggars on the steps of the mosque. Careless towards his own welfare, he assigned an ample allowance of five thousand pieces of silver to each of the aged warriors, the relics of the battle fields who had fought and protected the homeland of ages past.

Umar provides an ancient look into effective leadership then and today, those principles that served the people also serve our workers today.

Khalid bin al-Walid: The Sword of God

Khalid Walid is one of the few Muslim military generals in history to have the distinction of remained undefeated in battle their entire life. He has the distinction of being undefeated in over a hundred battles, against the numerically superior forces while insisting on unusual compassion and justice considering the times.

Walid converted to Islam and joined Muhammad after the Treaty of Hudaybiyyah and participated in various expeditions for him. After Muhammad's death, he played a key role in commanding forces in conquering central Arabia and subduing Arab tribes.

Khalid demonstrated unusual effective leadership qualities for his time, as an undefeated warrior, he was able to control his emotions and gain the confidence of others above him as well as below. An example of his coolness and control emerged when he was relieved of command by Umar as he had become a hero to the Muslims who attributed his successful wins of battles to his personality and presence; Umar the Leader of Muslims at the time was reported as saying: "I did not fire Khalid bin al Walid because I am angry with him or because of betrayal of trust or responsibility but the reason was that he was becoming a "idol" to the people and I wanted people to know that it is God who gives victory", this resulted in the dismissal of Khalid from supreme command and later in 638, from military services.

Khalid was not offended and gave a pledge of loyalty to Umar and continued service as an ordinary commander. There was inevitably a slowdown in the pace of military operations, as his replacements would move slowly and steadily and were more cautious commanders. The conquest of Syria continued under his Generalship and, Abu Ubaidah being an admirer of Khalid, gave him command of the cavalry and used him as a military advisor.

Khalid, by now, was at the height of his career, he was famous and loved by his men, for Muslim community he was a national hero, and was publicly known as **Sayf-ullah** (*Sword of Allah*).

Khalid's calmness, compassion and leading by example are a tribute to his character as a leader. His coolness under difficult situations can best be understood through an incident while in the heat of battle:

Khalid's Integrity in Battle

During a hard fought battle Khalid had taken a position with his troops at the front providing presence and encouragement to his troops, as the battle became intense, Khalid dismounted his horse and began to engage in fierce hand to hand fighting.

As the enemy was retreating, an enemy fighter was brought to him with the intent of execution at Khalid's hands, just as his sword was raised the captured fighter spit in his face at which Khalid lowered his sword and sheathed it and told the lucky soldier to leave the battle field and go home.

His astonished officers crowded around him asking why he had let the prisoner go. Khalid's response was simple. "I am fighting this war for God, if I had slain him; it would have because of my own anger and not for God."

Although it is believed that relations between Umar and Khalid, cousins, were always something short of cordial, Khalid apparently harbored no ill-will.

Upon his death, he bequeathed his property to Umar and made him the executor of his will and estate. Within less than four years of his dismissal, Khalid died and was buried in 642 in Emesa, where he lived since his dismissal from military services. He was quoted as saying:

> **I fought in so many battles seeking martyrdom that there is no place in my body but have a stabbing scar by a spear, a sword or a dagger, and yet here I am, dying on my bed like an old camel dies. May the eyes of the cowards never sleep.**
>
> **Khalid Whalid—The Sword of God**

When the news of Khalid's death reached the populace it broke like a storm over Medina. The women took to the streets wailing and beating their chests. Though the leadership from the very first day had given orders that there would be no wailing for departed Muslims, as forbidden in Islam, in this one case they made an exception. It was proclaimed:

> **Let the women say what they will about Abu Sulaiman (Khalid), for they do not lie, over the likes of Abu Sulaiman weep those who weep.**
>
> **Umar**

Khalid fought around a hundred battles, both major battles and minor skirmishes, during his military career. Having remained undefeated, this fact makes him one of the finest generals in history.

These two examples of Islamic leaders demonstrated all the following qualities of effective leadership recognized today:

Leadership	Character
Led by Example	Fairness
Good Judgment	Honesty
Knowledge	Initiative
Responsibility	Compassion
Teamwork	Modesty
Empathy	Sacrifice
Benevolence	Wisdom

Chapter 13

Comparing Leadership—The Military Leader

Can good military leaders become effective civilian leaders and vice versa? I am asked this question about my military background and the difference between military and civilian styles all the time. The answer based on research and my experience has always a clear "there is no difference in style". I have been met with curiosity, with cautiousness and in a few cases near contempt. I can usually answer all their questions and concerns after a few minutes and in most cases on departure have comments made such as "you don't have that hard starchy style."

It is expected by most people I meet that the military side of me will be firm, aggressive, commanding or even tyrannical. Most of my interviewers' are taken back with my explanation that there is no such thing as military vs. civilian "style" my argument and presentation is very simple, there are more similarities than differences. I have met tyrannical leaders in the military and in the civilian world as I have met leaders who are thoughtful and kind in both as well. The idealized characteristics for effective leadership that is found in non-military leaders are exactly the same for those who serve in and with the military.

What differences exist is found in the social and organizational culture of the organization itself, not the individual behaviors. The U.S. military has been around since The U.S. Army military manual of leadership, (FM 6-22) cite certain attributes that are universally prized: attention to detail, mission accomplishment, caring for subordinates, making the intent of the commander clear, physical and moral courage, and willingness to sacrifice for the larger cause both individual and collective. The challenges faced by leaders in the military and civilian sector become more similar the higher one moves up the organizational ladder. Groups in either system tend to share similar social values as well as ethics and understanding of styles and beliefs. Yet there are differences.

From the beginning of an officers career to include academy and civilian college pre-service years, military officers spend at least twice as much time in classrooms over their career as do their civilian equivalents. The education level of military officers above the rank of Captain tend to be higher than their civilian counterparts with 68 percent of military officers above the rank of Captain having a master's or higher degree, whereas about 20 percent of the corporate leaders have attained that level of formal education.

The main differences that civilians tend to confuse as "Militaristic" are nothing more than differences in the cultures that separate the two. The basis of the military culture begins when an emerging officer takes an oath (a promise), to defend and give both life and liberty if necessary to a higher cause than themselves. This is completely absent in the civilian culture, there is no initial expectation for commitment or sacrifice to the organization in the civilian culture. The expectation of personal sacrifice is key.

The military culture places a high degree of emphasis on personal character rather than on personal expertise. The civilian counterpart is usually valued for expertise placing character as a lower priority. For example, trustworthiness remains essential to both sectors but is more greatly prized as a military officer given the demanding circumstances typical of military operations and what is at stake. An example is when a highly knowledgeable Lieutenant is attacking a hill, he may know tactics and the right methods but if he is not trusted no one will follow him. Where in the civilian world where the stakes of losing life is not an issue, the executive who has low trust will still be followed. The bedrock of military of a military officer's reputation is "character."

Another cultural difference is belonging to something bigger than oneself in the military. There is only one military in our nation. There is no jumping to another military or jumping for different experiences as is the case in the civilian markets. The military offers one company;

it is the officer's entire profession. Within the military "company", there is great diversity to grow and expand. An officer will be called upon to be a front line supervisor, a logistical manager, transportation coordinator, purchasing agent, college professor and more all within the confines of the "company." Officers are promoted from within without any exceptions, there are no outside candidates. Every General has been a second lieutenant. Promotions decisions are centralized and everyone is on the same level playing field. Assignments are made regardless of race age or gender, which in turn lends to a strong sense of commitment and fairness. This movement up is not found in the civilian market.

Living within the military culture has a bonding effect on its members. Such things as sharing hardships over the years in far off lands and under inhospitable places; flying away in the dead of night with very little notice creates enduring ties creating a culture of sameness. It creates strong teams and binding feelings. This cohesion is a source of satisfaction and comfort, and the catalyst for teamwork.

In general, leadership in the military is different only because of its culture but the differences between civilian and military are over-stated. In both military and civilian worlds people rise to higher positions basically in similar fashion, through demonstration of skills and behaviors essential to organizational productivity and in harmony with the organizational culture. Good cultures and good leaders universally have similarities across both worlds and within the American society.

There is one outstanding factor that influences military officers over their civilian counterparts. Military officers are expected to die if necessary to accomplish the task at hand. This can create remarkable leadership situations not found with civilian leaders. While there are hundreds of examples, one example that stands out is that of Lt. Murphy who gave his life for a greater cause on June 28, 2005.

Lt. Murphy's Story

On June 28, 2005, deep behind enemy lines in Afghanistan, a four-man Navy SEAL team was conducting a reconnaissance mission at an altitude of approximately 10,000 feet high in the mountains. The team, Lt. Michael Murphy, Gunner's Mate

2nd Class (SEAL) Danny Dietz, Technician 2nd Class (SEAL) Matthew Axelson and Corpsman 2nd Class (SEAL) Marcus Luttrell had a vital task. The four team members were scouting Ahmad Shah—a terrorist in his mid-30s who grew up in the adjacent mountains just to the south.

The SEAL mission was compromised when the team was spotted by local nationals, who presumably reported its presence and location to the Taliban.

A fierce firefight erupted between the four team members and a much larger enemy force of more than fifty anti-coalition militia. The enemy had the team outnumbered. They also had terrain advantage. They launched a well-organized, three-sided attack on the teams. The firefight continued relentlessly as the overwhelming militia forced the team deeper into a ravine.

Trying to reach safety, the four men, each wounded, began bounding down the mountain's steep sides, making leaps of 20 to 30 feet. Approximately 45 minutes into the fight, pinned down by overwhelming forces, Dietz, the communications officer, sought open air to place a distress call back to the base. But before he could, he was shot in the hand, the blast shattering his thumb.

Despite the intensity of the firefight and suffering grave gunshot wounds himself, Murphy decided as the team leader to risk his own life to save the lives of his team. Murphy, intent on making contact with headquarters, but realizing this would be impossible in the extreme terrain where they were fighting, unhesitatingly and with complete disregard for his own life moved into the open, where he could gain a better position to transmit a call to get help for his men and seek emergency extraction from a difficult situation.

Moving away from the protective mountain rocks, he knowingly exposed himself to increased enemy gunfire. This deliberate and heroic act deprived him of cover and made him a target for the enemy. While continuing to be fired upon, Murphy made contact with the SOF Quick Reaction Force and requested assistance. He calmly went to a rock, sat down and provided his unit's location and the size of the enemy force while requesting immediate support for his team. At that point he was shot in the back causing him to drop the transmitter. Still sitting on the rock Murphy picked it back up, completed the call and continued firing at the enemy who was closing in. Lt. Murphy received sixteen mortal direct hits in his chest, head and back before slumping forward, his last remarks to the SOF operator was "—thank you—out".

An MH-47 Chinook helicopter, with eight additional members and eight Army Night Stalkers aboard, was sent is as part of an extraction mission to pull out the four embattled team. The MH-47 was escorted by heavily-armored, Army attack helicopters. Entering a hot combat zone, attack helicopters are used initially to neutralize the enemy and make it safer for the lightly-armored, personnel-transport helicopter, (Chinook), to insert.

The heavy weight of the attack helicopters slowed the formation's advance prompting the MH-47 to outrun their armored escort. They knew the tremendous risk going into an active enemy area in daylight, without their attack support, and without the cover of night. Risk would, of course, be minimized if they put the helicopter down in a safe zone.

But knowing that their warrior brothers were shot, surrounded and severely wounded, the rescue team opted to directly enter the oncoming battle in hopes of landing on brutally hazardous terrain. As the Chinook raced to the battle, a rocket-propelled grenade struck the helicopter, killing all 16 men aboard. On the ground and nearly out of ammunition, the remaining members, Luttrell, Dietz and Axelson, continued the fight. By the end of the two-hour gunfight that careened through the hills and over cliffs, Axelson and Dietz had been killed. An estimated 35 Taliban who were engaged in the attack were also dead or dying.

The fourth SEAL, Luttrell, was blasted over a ridge by a rocket propelled grenade and was knocked unconscious. Regaining consciousness some time later, Luttrell managed to escape—badly injured—and slowly crawl away down the side of a cliff. Dehydrated, with a bullet wound to one leg, shrapnel embedded in both legs, three vertebrae cracked; the situation for Luttrell was grim. Rescue helicopters were sent in, but he was too weak and injured to make contact. Traveling seven miles on foot he evaded the enemy for nearly a day. Gratefully, local nationals came to his aid, carrying him to a nearby village where they kept him for three days. The Taliban came to the village several times demanding that Luttrell be turned over to them. The villagers refused. One of the villagers made his way to a Marine outpost with a note from Luttrell, and U.S. forces launched a massive operation that rescued him from enemy territory on July 2.

Leadership at its extreme with demonstrated initiative, persistence, commitment, from a group of men whom had been relatively carefree civilians just years earlier. The difference now was shared values that were seen by all them as worthy sacrifice. This level of commitment is very seldom seen in the civilian world but reflects the difference based on culture.

Business and civilian occupations is not war, nor should the two be confused as preferred, it is simply a matter of situational context. The non-military world draws from the same resources as does the military, the difference is a matter of culture, building leadership pools and ultimately being able to build commitment to the organization, a commitment that can sustain creative independent action and is the secret to great leaders.

In both war and peace, in or out of the military, effective leadership comes down to character, behavior and respect for our fellow people. Winning the battle is not as important as how you fought the battle.

Conclusion

Leadership positions do not totally protect us from temptation or from making mistakes, but how we act and what we say is what makes the difference.

10 Points of Leadership Fundamentals

LEADERSHIP FUNDAMENTAL 1
Good leaders understand the worth of the individual

When people are hired into an organization, we hire them because they have demonstrated certain abilities and have proved themselves at other organizations or businesses. What leaders must understand is that every person is different; they bring different talents, abilities and personalities. Understanding these differences help us to see in others what otherwise would be missed. Good leaders see people for not what they are now but for what they can become and act on that.

I recall a time when I was in the process of buying a horse for my children. I went to the local auction house on a hot summer day in Oklahoma. I arrived late, and all of the good horses had already been sold. The few that remained were old and spent and had been bought by a company that would slaughter them for export to Europe. I was about to leave when one of these horses—an uncared-for, large Belgium with scares on its side and hips—caught my eye. The animal still bore the marks that had been made by abuse and perhaps the hard life he had led. But something about him captured my attention, so I offered $500 for him.

It was a very hot day when my children saw the horse for the first time, and because of the heat, his coat was wet and looked like wet sand, the children named him "Sandy." I took good care of the horse, which turned out to be a gentle and reliable friend—a horse the girls liked to ride because he was steady and didn't startle like some of the others. In fact, Sandy made such rapid improvement that my neighbor purchased him for twice what I had originally paid. But Sandy kept disappearing from the neighbor's pasture—sometimes ending up in adjoining fields, other times back at my place. It appeared that the horse must have pushed over the fence between the properties, but that seemed impossible—I had never seen Sandy push through anything, but eventually, the neighbor's patience came to an end, and he insisted I take back the horse.

For years, I wanted to participate in sled pulling contests but never felt that I could afford to buy a pedigreed horse that had been specifically bred to pull. Sandy was already getting old—he was nine when I had purchased him—and he had been badly treated. But, apparently, Sandy wanted to pull, so I decided to see what the horse could do. What I saw made me think that maybe Sandy had a chance to compete. I entered Sandy in his first competition. Sandy stood among the beautifully bred, champion horses, looking very much out of place, especially with his sagging back and scares on his side. Other horse breeders called Sandy a broken old hunk. A wonderful, unbelievable thing happened that day. Sandy won! I continued to enter Sandy in other competitions, and Sandy continued to win. Audiences cheered every time Sandy won an event. He became a symbol of how extraordinary an ordinary horse could be. He became a local celebrity and was used on hay rides and local fairs. As Sandy continued to win, one buyer offered $10,000 for the old horse, but I could not sell. Later that year, Sandy was nominated for "Horse of the Year." The old Belgium who had once been marked for sale to a low bidder and who was on his way to the slaughter house had become a champion.

Several months later on a cold winters morning and before his nomination was final, I found Sandy lying on his side near an old Oak tree. As I laid my hand on his cold body I slumped beside him with deep sadness. I had lost more than a champion horse, I had lost a friend who trusted me and in return gave me and my family many hours of companionship and happiness. But what Sandy really gave me was what he represented; he became an example of the hidden, untapped potential that lies within each of us.

Leaders must understand the power of individual talent and ensuring the success of the individual by seeking their best interest and know that it will benefit the group and the organization. However, in the business world, taking care of the individual and group, may often mean that those above or around you may become angry at your actions and decisions. They tend to demand quick or harsh action, termination for those who make one mistake or demand reprimand type actions. It's inevitable if you maintain your courage. Having the courage to confront those who would diminish your style and team building efforts will be hard at times, but those who work for you and see your genuine efforts, will not let you down.

LEADERSHIP FUNDAMENTAL 2
Effective leadership is all about trust

During the Revolutionary War, Washington had control of the army and may have been able to use its power for his own political gain. Indeed, after the fighting had ended, some men tried to use the army to make Washington king. When Washington learned of this, he went to Newburgh, Connecticut, to speak to the army officers.

Keep in mind that Washington was not an orator. Years later when he gave his first inaugural address as president of the United States, he delivered the speech so poorly that few even knew what he said until the next day when it was published in the newspapers. In Newburgh it was different. When one reads the speech, it does not seem so overwhelming—he simply reminded them that they had been fighting for their freedom and said that he would "spurn" any attempt to distort that freedom. But his simple speech "drew tears" from the war-hardened officers who heard him and dissolved the conspiracy.

It speaks well of Washington that those who wanted a king trusted his ability to be king but that is only half the story. Several years later, when the new Constitution was being debated, many people feared it gave too much power to the president. One reason they were willing to vote for the ratification of the Constitution was because they knew that Washington would become our first president and believed they could trust him with that much power.

Throughout his career Washington was aware of the significance of the role he played. "It has been a kind of destiny that has thrown me upon this service," he once confided to his wife. "I shall hope that my undertaking it is designed to answer some good purpose."

Developing trust between people is the keystone to leadership success. When your workers stop bringing you their problems is the day you have stopped leading them. Losing workers trust and their confidence that you can help them is catastrophic.

When workers leave an organization it is usually because of failed leadership at the front line, workers leave bosses not organizations. The link to failed trust usually begins when bosses build barriers to upward communication and create a culture or mindset, that the very idea of someone lower in the hierarchy looking up to the leader for help is seen as a weakness. As result, workers do not share critical information that leads to awareness and necessary change. Effective leaders are always accessible and available. They care and are genuinely concerned for the efforts and challenges faced by those who work for them and nearly always, the results are that a team is built and creative problem solving replaces finger pointing and blame.

LEADERSHIP FUNDAMENTAL 3
Leaders are not afraid to do the unexpected.

Good leaders do not follow the fads and management trends, they do the unexpected but they learn their trade and become skilled at what they do, they seek out people who have character to help build and become partners, because they understand that it is easy to train skills, it is difficult to train character. Break free of hieratical restrictions; be careful not to become a slave to policy and procedures that compel you to lead by blind obedience to the system. Good leaders don't wait for official blessing to try things out; they know when to do the unexpected but with good judgment and are never reckless.

LEADERSHIP FUNDAMENTAL 4
Do not be afraid to set high standards and never neglect details.

Setting high standards helps people become better as long as mistakes are allowed and tempered with constructive advice and correction. Setting high standards requires leaders to delegate and empower others liberally, but ensure that details are part of the standards. At the same time, good leaders expect and encourage people to challenge the process and look for the better way.

LEADERSHIP FUNDAMENTAL 5
Attracting and retaining good talent makes for success.

Machines and systems cannot replace human assets; only people can bring the versatility, talents, creativity and the "what it takes" attitude to an organization. Too often, people are assumed to be mindless walking muscles that are to be used by those who have an omnipotent attitude. Good leaders avoid this pit at all costs and make time to immerse themselves in the goal of creating an environment where the best, the brightest, the most creative are attracted, retained and-most importantly-unleashed. They get to know the people, even making them their friends.

LEADERSHIP FUNDAMENTAL 6
Leaders create the round table—Let people participate

King Author sat his knights around a table that was not square but round. He wanted those who followed him to understand that there was no one among them better than the other or set apart from the other. They were all equal and were required to face each other squarely, signifying there equality in all things but more importantly to make each aware of their obligation and accountability to each other as a team. There were no organization charts, no paintings of the top men, just each other. Leaders who really understand leadership know that titles are meaningless. At best, they advertise some authority—an official status conferring the ability to give orders and induce obedience.

Rather, they understand that real power and influence comes by free will and is a gift to the leader from the people, it is unexpected and unsolicited. People will personally commit to leaders who have ability, integrity and benevolence, who genuinely care for others interests even above their own. Ineffective leaders on the other hand, may be anointed with titles and position but it guarantees them no respect or commitment from the workers.

It is my experience that most workers who are led by poor leaders will nearly always respect the position but not necessarily the person in that position or holding the title. Respect and influence must be earned and for leaders who never receive that respect at best may be able to extract minimal compliance to minimal standards.

LEADERSHIP FUNDAMENTAL 7
Good leaders are themselves and they know who they are

Effective leaders understand that the latest trends such as TQM, participative management; leader member exchange and all the other management hot topics can be confusing and short lived. Following basic leadership principles and knowing who you are usually is enough to generate the motivation necessary for effective team building. I have walked into too many workplaces that have faded hangings of logos or bullet points representing dead programs that were blindly followed by upper leadership but could not be sustained because the particular fad generated rigidity in thought and action.

There are times when a flat out directive is more appropriate than participatory discussion. Good leaders know when to bear down with firm yet tempered decisions, when some situations require the leader to hover closely and when direction is minimal.

LEADERSHIP FUNDAMENTAL 8
Creates a positive environment

Leaders must be positive and uplifting—keeping in mind that letting others maintain a strong self-esteem motivates.

An organization's climate springs from its leader's attitudes, actions, and priorities. These are engrained through choices, policies, and programs. Once in an organizational leadership position, the leader determines the organizational climate by assessing the organization from the bottom up. Once this assessment is done, the leader can provide clear guidance and focus (purpose, direction, and motivation) to move the organization towards the desired end state. He must work at creating a climate that promotes values, encourages learning, promotes creativity and establishes cohesion. However, the foundation for a positive environment is a healthy ethical climate that is established by the leader's example in all areas of his office.

To create such a climate, organizational leaders recognize mistakes as opportunities to learn, create cohesive teams, and reward leaders of character and competence with increasing responsibilities. Organizational leaders value honest feedback and constantly use all available means to maintain a feel for the organization within the contemporary operational environment. Special staff members who may be good sources for quality feedback include Human Resources and your front line leaders. The organizational leader's feedback methods include group meetings, surveys, and councils.

The example a leader sets creates the working environment. Leaders who criticize, condemn and complain will foster the same behavior among the group. Criticism and condemnation diminish eagerness and excitement. Leaders who understand this principle will be smart to seek workers and team members who have a strong character, it is easy to train skills but it is nearly impossible to train people to have integrity, judgment, kindness and benevolence. Hire optimism over pessimism always.

LEADERSHIP FUNDAMENTAL 9
Effective leaders seldom lose their temper or argue.

Leaders use effective communications which are expressions of affection and not anger, facts and not fabrication, compassion and not contention, respect and not ridicule, counsel and not criticism, correction and not condemnation. Their words are spoken with clarity and not with confusion. They may be tender or they may be tough, but they must always be tempered. When a leader loses his temper or encourages an argument, at that moment he loses respect and commitment from those around him.

The size of a leader may be measured by the size of the things that make him angry. To become upset and infuriated over trivial matters gives evidence of childishness and immaturity in a leader. Not only does intemperate anger affect leaders physically and mentally, in a negative way, but at the same time it also destroys wisdom and sound judgment. When we become upset, reason is suppressed, and anger rushes in. To make decisions while infuriated is as unwise and foolish as it is for a captain to put out to sea in a raging storm. Only injury and wreckage result from wrathful moments.

When anger rules, tempered judgment flees. Actually, the leader who is composed has a distinct advantage over one who is angered. When a leader is in the right, he need not lose his temper; and when he is wrong, he cannot afford to. Anger against *things* is senseless indeed! Because a clerk failed to order a necessary part and a critical piece of equipment is down, is no reason for throwing the clipboard halfway across the office. Having a load of product sent back to be re-worked during a busy week will not be remedied by a tirade of words. Anger against *things* is bad enough, but when it is directed against people and it flares up with white-hot fury and caustic words, we have the makings of tragedy! For example, when a leader loses control of his or her temper and becomes angry in a meeting, the impact is immediate; all eagerness is diminished, there will be very little exchange of ideas and if there is it will be comments that are agreeable and safe. Another example, let some selfish driver cut in too close in front of another car as he passes, and then let the offended driver fail to reduce his speed and angrily "tailgate," or do something else "to get even"; then a tragedy is in the making.

For a leader to lose his or her temper, to explode, to become ugly, punitive, and hateful when faced with frustrations is inexcusable! Why is it inexcusable to explode with anger and become vindictive? Simply because the power has been given us to control and to overcome such tendencies. If not curbed, such tendencies soon lose for us the leader, respect and trust of others.

There are arguments that some of these characteristics are too ambiguous and that there are degrees of competencies. I would argue this—You Know—. You either are or you have struggled with one or all. Answer it without debate; give it your unbiased true view. Remember: You know.

No one is perfect, nor will we be, but we can stretch ourselves to reach perfection and improve on these characteristics so that we become meaningful to others. Knowing your weaknesses and acting to improve them takes courage. Knowing your weaknesses and doing nothing to improve is arrogance.

Acknowledgment

This book would not have been possible without the support of many people to include my wife Suzanne, my five children and my parents. Special thanks also to all my work associates and friends for their ongoing support and being tolerant of my seemingly endless questioning. In particular, I am indebted to Khalid Otaibi who models Transformational Leadership and who made my life enjoyable and meaningful far away from home surrounded by a different culture.

My heartfelt thanks to my wife Suzanne and daughter Charmaine, two seasoned English teachers who on countless nights providing editorial support.

I express my gratitude to Ed Faro the books photo editor whose amazing technical skills brought to life old photos. Ed's professionalism and dedication to this project is deeply appreciated

Finally, for Crystal, Samuel, Annette, and Barbara who provide endless encouragement and advice; no words can express my love and gratitude.

Military Photos

3rd Platoon A Company DMZ Korea—Author is center Left
seated on box.

A Company—Camp liberty Bell Korea DMZ

SFC Roy Evans—1979 DMZ Korea

Dr. Shelton right, preparing to overfly the DMZ for night operation

El Real forward base along Columbian border

Panamanian Defense Force at El Real base.
Captain Feeny second from left Logistics Officer

Zodiacs from LCM taking supplies forward base at El Real

Captain Shelton far right standing at the War College with Chilean
staff Santiago Chili

Captain Morales standing in front of the National Stadium Santiago
Chile where an estimated 10,000 Chilean citizens
were interrogated, tortured and executed.

Captain Morales second from left and my wife Suzanne holding our daughter Annette third from left. Flying to Del Mar Chili.

Dr. Shelton with Senator Ike Skelton, School of Americas, Panama

Penn State Photos

Dr. Shelton second from right with his class during the Caledonia
Bay Leadership Exercise—Author in background

Penn State students trekking in the Darien Jungle of South America

Khalid Otaibi and Dr. Shelton delivering a presentation at a
international conference on Leadership in The Kingdom of Bahrain

Supervisor Pocket Guide
from Leadership

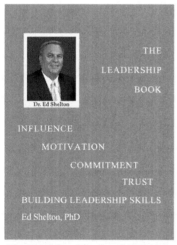

The Golden Leadership Book

Dr. EDWARD J. SHELTON

The Leadership Book

Dr. Shelton shares some popular quotes from the book in this condensed pocket sized book. Powerful thoughts that remind us of preferred leadership behaviors and actions. The focus is on communications, engagement, motivation and trust.

Contact Dr. Shelton at shelton.acla@yahoo.com

Made in the USA
Middletown, DE
01 December 2015